Building a Successful Palestinian State

Security

Robert E. Hunter, Seth G. Jones

Supported by a gift from David and Carol Richards

RAND
CORPORATION

Research for this study was carried out between September 2002 and July 2005 under the direction of the RAND Health Center for Domestic and International Health Security in conjunction with the Center for Middle East Public Policy (CMEPP), one of RAND's international programs. RAND Health and CMEPP are units of the RAND Corporation. Primary funding for this study was provided by a generous gift from David and Carol Richards. This research in the public interest was also supported by RAND, using discretionary funds made possible by the generosity of RAND's donors and the earnings on client-funded research.

Library of Congress Cataloging-in-Publication Data

Hunter, Robert Edwards, 1940-
    Building a successful Palestinian state : security / Robert E. Hunter, Seth G. Jones.
      p. ; cm.
    "MG-146/2."
    Includes bibliographical references.
    ISBN 0-8330-3811-7 (pbk. : alk. paper)
    1. Arab-Israeli conflict—1993—Peace. 2. Palestinian Arabs—Politics and government. 3. National security—Israel. I. Jones, Seth G., 1972– II. Title.

    DS119.76.H84 2006
    956.05'3—dc22
                                                                                            2005034076

The RAND Corporation is a nonprofit research organization providing objective analysis and effective solutions that address the challenges facing the public and private sectors around the world. RAND's publications do not necessarily reflect the opinions of its research clients and sponsors.

RAND® is a registered trademark.

Published 2006 by the RAND Corporation
1776 Main Street, P.O. Box 2138, Santa Monica, CA 90407-2138
1200 South Hayes Street, Arlington, VA 22202-5050
201 North Craig Street, Suite 202, Pittsburgh, PA 15213-1516
RAND URL: http://www.rand.org/
To order RAND documents or to obtain additional information, contact
Distribution Services: Telephone: (310) 451-7002;
Fax: (310) 451-6915; Email: order@rand.org

Preface

For the last three years, the RAND Corporation has undertaken a major project focused on a single question: How can an independent Palestinian state be made successful? This project has analyzed and discussed a wide range of issues, from demographics and economics to health care and education. The results have been presented in four RAND publications: *Building a Successful Palestinian State* (The RAND Palestinian State Study Team, 2005); *The Arc: A Formal Structure for a Palestinian State* (Suisman et al., 2005); *Helping a Palestinian State Succeed: Key Findings* (2005); and *Strengthening the Palestinian Health System* (Schoenbaum, Afifi, and Deckelbaum, 2005).

This study examines key security issues regarding the construction of a Palestinian state. Throughout the history of Arab-Israeli peace negotiations, security has been the most important—and most challenging—issue for Palestinians, Israelis, and their neighbors. Indeed, security trumps all in terms of the requirements of turning war to peace and conflict to potential cooperation. *Building a Successful Palestinian State* dealt with matters of security *within* an independent Palestinian state. This study addresses the *external* security of such a state. External security clearly has many dimensions and requires, first and foremost, a thorough examination of the attitudes, analyses, ideas, and needs of the two critical parties: Israel and Palestine. Analysis of external security requirements also calls for examining relations of an independent Palestinian state with its neighbors, the role of outside powers and key international institutions, and the political and security picture of the Middle East as a whole.

As with other aspects of the overall RAND Palestinian project, this study does not prescribe means for getting from the situation today to the establishment of a Palestinian state. Nor does it include a discussion of what a final status agreement should look like, except to the extent that consideration of the role of security issues in negotiations is indispensable for a successful outcome. The focus here is instead on what, in the authors' judgment, would need to be done in terms of external security so that the key parties, especially Israelis and Palestinians, can have high confidence that a peace agreement can be sustained. The study does not attempt to recount the negotiations that have been conducted over the past several decades, but rather focuses on those critical elements—

such as border arrangements, Israeli settlements, a role (if any) for Palestinian military forces, and confidence-building and security-enhancing measures of all types—that have emerged in the history of efforts to bring this conflict to a close.

Research for this study was carried out between September 2002 and July 2005 under the direction of the RAND Health Center for Domestic and International Health Security in conjunction with the Center for Middle East Public Policy (CMEPP), one of RAND's international programs. RAND Health and CMEPP are units of the RAND Corporation.

Primary funding for this study was provided by a generous gift from David and Carol Richards, and the authors are deeply indebted to them for their inspiration, vision, and support. This research in the public interest was also supported by RAND, using discretionary funds made possible by the generosity of RAND's donors and the earnings on client-funded research.

Contents

Preface iii

Figures and Tables vii

Summary ix

1. Introduction 1

2. Border Arrangements 7

3. International Force 13

4. Palestinian Military Forces 27

5. Israeli Settlements 33

6. Intelligence, Monitoring, Enforcement, and Dispute-Resolution Provisions 37

7. Special Security Issues Regarding Jerusalem 41

8. External Security Environment 45

9. Conclusion 49

Appendix

A. Security Issues and the Arab-Israeli Peace Process, 1967–2003 51

B. "Clinton Parameters" (Presented by President Bill Clinton
   to the Israeli and Palestinian Negotiators on December 23, 2000) 63

Bibliography 69

Figures and Tables

Figures

1. Security Fence Route Approved by the Israeli Government, February 20, 2005 9
2. Israeli Settlements in the West Bank 34

Tables

1. Peacekeeping Missions in the Middle East, 1948–2003 14
2. Per-Year Costs for a Palestinian Peace-Enabling Force 26

Summary

This monograph examines the requirements and key options for external security following the conclusion of an Israeli-Palestinian peace accord and the creation of a Palestinian state. It is presented in association with the RAND Corporation study, *Building a Successful Palestinian State* (The RAND Palestinian State Study Team, 2005). Internal and external security arrangements for a Palestinian state are inextricably related. Examples include the effectiveness of Palestinian policing and the nature and extent of security arrangements along the Palestinian-Israeli border, counterterrorism efforts, and intelligence functions. Thus, the discussion in this study necessarily overlaps the issues presented in the broader study. It focuses primarily on security issues that involve borders and direct interaction between Palestine and its neighbors. We also assume that whatever agreement is reached will be consonant with the so-called two-state solution.

At the same time, this study is designed to describe, analyze, and discuss key issues related to the external security of a Palestinian state following the achievement of peace between Israel and Palestine. It thus does not seek to examine all issues in light of the negotiating history, since that history may or may not have an impact on the situation prevailing during a state of peace. Thus, possibilities for security arrangements that have so far proved to be unacceptable to one party or the other might be viewed in a different light during peacetime. This study seeks to present a series of useful and reasonable steps, but not to evaluate how "negotiable" they might be in future circumstances that obviously cannot be accurately forecast. Similarly, while referring to some important past ideas, this study does not attempt to review the full history of discussions, debates, and negotiations on security issues between Israelis and Palestinians, and there have been many such. For a historical account, the reader is invited to see the literature on the subject. This includes, for example, works by past U.S. negotiators William Quandt (during the Carter administration) and Dennis Ross (1988–2000).[1] Furthermore, Appendix B contains the text of the proposals made to the Israelis and Palestinians by President Bill Clinton in December 2000.

---

[1] See, in particular, Quandt (2001a); and Ross (2004).

In recent months,[2] the prospects for peace between Israel and a potential Palestinian state have taken a positive turn. Following the death of Yasser Arafat in November 2004, elections for a new president (Mahmoud Abbas) of the Palestinian Authority were held in the Occupied Territories in January 2005. Israel has withdrawn from Gaza and a few Israeli settlements in the northern West Bank. The second Bush administration recommitted itself to the pursuit of peacemaking and sent Lieutenant General William Ward to assist with Israel's disengagement from Gaza and to help train, equip, and advise Palestinian security forces. The people of Lebanon have risen against Syrian occupation, and Syria has been required to withdraw its forces and intelligence apparatus. And there is broad international support, including by the so-called Quartet (the United States, the European Union, the United Nations, and the Russian Federation) for renewed peace efforts based on the Roadmap.[3] Of course, this does not mean that a peace agreement is imminent. But it does mean that considerations about the requirements for implementing such an agreement—including requirements for the external security of both Israel and a Palestinian state—have gained new saliency. Further, while it is not the objective of this study to analyze or prescribe alternatives for actual peace negotiations, the issues discussed here will certainly be germane to those negotiations and can help inform decisions to be made by the Israelis and the Palestinians.

Ideas presented here need to be evaluated as possible elements of a settlement that itself would have to be agreed upon for these ideas to come into play. What we describe are the conditions for success if the "possible" does become possible. Indeed, at such moments, forethought becomes particularly important as a tool of statecraft, helping opportunities to be seized.

This study offers several general conclusions:

- *Primacy of Security:* Security trumps all else. Without it—as demonstrated by several decades of experience in Arab-Israeli peacemaking, including every agreement between Israel and one or more of its neighbors since 1949—nothing else is likely to succeed in Israeli-Palestinian relations. Security considerations, therefore, must come first.

- *Security Is Indivisible:* Internal and external security issues for Israel and Palestine are inseparable, and both must be considered, organized, and implemented together. In addition to material contained here on internal security, readers are thus invited to refer to the companion document, *Building a Successful Palestinian State.*

---

[2] This study was completed in August 2005.

[3] See U.S Department of State (2003b).

- *Permeable Borders:* Assuming implementation of critical security measures, the Israeli-Palestinian border should be permeable, with checkpoints and inspections managed jointly by Israel and Palestine. If both parties agree, performance of these tasks could usefully be assisted by a U.S.-led international force.

- *International Force:* Following a peace settlement and subject to agreement by Israel and Palestine, a U.S.-led international peace-enabling force should be deployed along the Palestinian borders with Egypt, Jordan, and Israel—including along potential borders in Jerusalem. Its objectives should include supervising the withdrawal of Israeli forces from Palestinian territory, helping to monitor and patrol border crossings, supervising further measures of de-escalation after a peace settlement, and engaging in other duties agreed upon by all parties. This force could be limited in size (perhaps ranging from 2,500 to 7,000 troops).[4] It must have clear and precise rules of engagement; and it should have an open-ended mandate, but with the goal of being limited in duration.

- *NATO's Role*: If Israel and Palestine agree, this U.S.-led international force could usefully be based on NATO and also include forces from other countries, pursuant to a formal UN Security Council mandate.

- *Peace First*: A peace settlement should be a precondition for deploying this force. While logic could argue for such a force to be created to buttress security following Israeli withdrawal from Gaza or to test principles and practices of an international force in this limited sphere, potential contributing countries would be unlikely to become engaged, at least with more than the European police on the Gaza-Egypt border, until there is an Israeli-Palestinian peace agreement.

- *Cost:* RAND estimates that the cost of a peace-enabling force might range from $550 million per year for a force of 2,500 soldiers, to $1.5 billion for 7,000 soldiers. Over ten years, these costs could range from $5 billion to $15 billion.

- *Palestinian Military Force*: Palestine should agree not to constitute regular military forces, certainly at first, although it should have border guards, police, and other domestic security forces. An increasing number of security responsibilities should be devolved upon the Palestinian government and its security forces over a five-to-ten-

---

[4] Estimates of troop levels in this study depend on assumptions about the security environment, rules of engagement, objectives, and operational tasks of the forces, and thus are included for the purpose of giving some sense of the magnitude of the obligations to be assumed. See later discussion. The number could be considerably larger under different assumptions.

year period, depending on proved competence and Israeli confidence. Whether Palestine should be permanently "demilitarized" is an issue to be considered at a later point, depending in part on events and on the nature of Israel-Palestine relations.

- *Israeli Settlements:* In order to maximize security, Israeli settlements within the borders of a Palestinian state should be withdrawn, except in territories that are contiguous to Israel proper and agreed upon in negotiations (e.g., potentially through land swaps).

- *Dispute-Resolution Mechanisms:* Joint Israeli-Palestinian dispute-resolution mechanisms will be a critical part of promoting security, possibly with international participation.

- *Jerusalem*: The status of Jerusalem is largely a political question. From a security perspective, Jerusalem can be the capital for both Israel and Palestine. Again, from a security perspective, there could be international aspects, especially in regard to the Temple Mount/Haram al-Sharif, with either mixed Israeli-Palestinian control or participation of outsiders.

- *Regional Security Environment:* Security for Israel and Palestine will depend to a critical degree on what else is happening in the Middle East. An overall Arab-Israeli settlement will be important. The United States has now taken on primary responsibility for reshaping the region and for developing long-term stability. Others, including NATO, the European Union, and the United Nations must also play useful and supportive roles.

1. Introduction

Every negotiation and plan for peace between Israel and its neighbors has had one overriding element—those issues and concerns that can be subsumed under the blanket term "security." Indeed, a wide spectrum of issues, ranging from economics and education to political governance, has bowed before security concerns in the course of efforts to create a just and lasting peace. Security trumps everything else. For this principal reason, there has been no major success at what, in many other parts of the world, have proved to be functional approaches to peace and resolution of conflict. Examples include mutual increases in standards of living that lead individuals, families, and communities to reduce if not eliminate their preoccupation with "security" and to put aside historical grievances and rival claims.[1] In time, that may happen with Israel and its neighbors, as well, including the Palestinians. But that day is some way off and will depend, among other things, on each party's sense of security. Thus, security issues will continue to have primacy in the effort to design the parameters of a viable Palestinian state. Other aspects of state creation, with few exceptions, will need to be related to these issues and the ways in which they are worked out.

Security issues will play a fundamental role in the creation of a Palestinian state in at least four overlapping ways. First, a Palestinian state must be able, alone or in concert with others, to ensure security within its own borders, consistent also with Israel's security. This includes the Palestinian state's ability to promote public order and to protect its citizens—as well as to protect others, either resident in or visiting its territory—from violent attack and subversion, whether originating from without or within the state, and to provide its citizens with a sense of normality in their daily lives. (The major issues involved with internal security are fully elaborated in the main RAND Corporation study (The RAND Palestinian State Study Team, 2005.)) Second, a Palestinian state must also take steps to enter into arrangements that will help to ensure Israel's security. These must

---

[1] This has been a central premise behind developments in Western Europe since the end of World War II, beginning with the Marshall Plan, the Organisation for Economic Co-operation and Development, NATO, and the European Union, and more recently, behind efforts to integrate Central European states in Euro-Atlantic political and economic as well as security institutions.

include credible reassurances through confidence-building measures, dispute-resolution provisions, and concrete steps to eliminate terrorist and other violent attacks against Israel originating from Palestinian territory. Third, the territories of both Israel and Palestine must be secured against incursion from abroad. Fourth, the creation of a Palestinian state must be seen as making a positive contribution to regional security—a goal that imposes burdens more on other states and institutions than on the Palestinian state, its institutions, and its leaders.

Designing a Palestinian state that can fulfill these four basic requirements—on its own, in cooperation with others, and in terms of its existence and relations with Israel and others—has historically proved to be beyond reach for a variety of reasons that we explore below. The challenge now is to analyze and explore each of these elements, along with their relationship to one another and to other key aspects of designing and creating a Palestinian state that can succeed.

Internal and external security arrangements for a Palestinian state are inextricably related. Examples include the effectiveness of Palestinian policing and the nature and extent of security arrangements along the Palestinian-Israeli border, counterterrorism efforts, and intelligence functions. Thus, the discussion in this monograph overlaps the issues presented in the companion RAND study. Both explore the relationships and overlap where it seems most appropriate to do so.

This monograph focuses on the external security dimensions of a Palestinian state (i.e., issues involving borders or direct interaction between a Palestinian state and its neighbors). We begin with a brief historical overview of major security issues since the 1993 Oslo Accords. We then offer analysis and options in those areas that we believe are central to external security concerns.

Historical Overview

Security concerns have been a *sine qua non* throughout the history of the Israeli-Palestinian peace process. This subsection outlines the major security agreements and negotiations since the 1993 Oslo Accords.[2] Oslo was an important step toward the creation of a Palestinian state because it transferred to the Palestine Liberation Organization (PLO) practical control over a small amount of territory in Gaza and the town of Jericho, along with the prospect that negotiations would proceed to a successful conclusion.[3]

---

[2] *Declaration of Principles on Interim Self-Government Arrangements* (1993).

[3] Israel officially recognized the PLO as the legitimate representative of the Palestinian people in a letter from Israeli Prime Minister Yitzhak Rabin to PLO Chairman Yasser Arafat on September 9, 1993. As William Quandt noted: "True, the territory was entirely surrounded by Israelis, was minute in size, and was teeming with economically distressed Palestinians. It was a start, however." Quandt (2001a), pp. 328–329.

The 1993 Oslo Accords and the subsequent 1994 Israel-PLO *Agreement on the Gaza Strip and the Jericho Area* were the first steps toward Palestinian sovereignty, and they included several important security elements. First, although the Palestinians acquired authority over Gaza and Jericho, Israel continued to have authority over Israeli settlements, military installations, and Israelis living within Palestinian territory.[4] Second, the Palestinian Authority was explicitly prohibited from exercising functional jurisdiction in the areas of foreign relations and external security. As Article VI of the 1994 Israel-PLO agreement stated:

> The Palestinian Authority will not have powers and responsibilities in the sphere of foreign relations, which sphere includes the establishment abroad of embassies, consulates or other types of foreign missions and posts or permitting their establishment in the Gaza Strip or Jericho Area, the appointment of or admission of diplomatic and consular staff, and the exercise of diplomatic functions.[5]

This provision ensured that Israel would monitor and secure the Palestinian borders with Egypt and Jordan, as well as defend against threats from the air and Mediterranean Sea. The Palestinians were prohibited from establishing a military and acquiring such equipment as heavy weapons and tanks, and their police forces were limited in the number and caliber of arms and ammunition they could possess. Third, the agreements created a series of bilateral and multilateral enforcement and monitoring arrangements that involved the Palestinian Authority, Israel, Jordan, Egypt, and the United States.[6] For example, the Israelis and Palestinians established a joint security coordination and cooperation committee for mutual security purposes, district coordination offices, and joint patrols. Liaison and cooperation arrangements were also established, involving the governments of Jordan and Egypt. In sum, following Oslo, Israel retained responsibility and authority over most internal and external security matters with regard to the West Bank and Gaza.

The situation did not change significantly over the next few years. However, two agreements were reached that were important *vis-à-vis* Palestinian and regional security: the 1994 Israel-Jordan Peace Treaty and the 1995 *Israeli-Palestinian Interim Agreement on the West Bank and the Gaza Strip* (Oslo II).[7] In most security areas, the status quo

---

[4] *Agreement on the Gaza Strip and the Jericho Area* (1994), Article V.

[5] *Agreement on the Gaza Strip and the Jericho Area* (1994), Article VI. Authority would only be transferred to the Palestinians in the spheres of education and culture, health, social welfare, taxation, and tourism. Also see *Declaration of Principles on Interim Self-Government Arrangements* (1993), Article VIII and Annex II.

[6] On Israeli-Palestinian arrangements, see *Agreement on the Gaza Strip and the Jericho Area* (1994), Annex I. On the involvement of Jordan and Egypt, see *Declaration of Principles on Interim Self-Government Arrangements* (1993); *Agreement on the Gaza Strip and the Jericho Area* (1994), Article XVI.

[7] *The (Oslo II) Interim Accord,* September 28, 1995. See http://www.usembassy-israel.org.il/publish/peace/interim.htm.

persisted, and Israel retained responsibility for external security. As Article XII of Oslo II stated: "Israel shall continue to carry the responsibility for defense against external threats, including the responsibility for protecting the Egyptian and Jordanian borders and for defense against external threats from the sea and air."[8] Israel retained responsibility for the security of Israeli settlements, military installations, and Israelis in Palestinian territory. The Palestinian Authority was again prohibited from establishing embassies and consulates abroad, creating a diplomatic staff, or building a military. Oslo II did give the Palestinian police power to maintain security and public order in most matters in Palestinian territory.[9] Oslo II also permitted the Palestinian Authority to make international agreements in the areas of financial aid, regional development, culture, science, and education.[10]

Another important change to the status quo was the Israel-Jordan Peace Treaty of October 1994, which contributed to a more peaceful regional security environment. In addition to establishing peace, Israel and Jordan agreed to cooperate in a number of areas: drug trafficking, counterterrorism, criminal activity, and border crossing.[11] The treaty was also important because it contributed to a more stable external security environment and provided for Jordanian involvement in the Israeli-Palestinian peace process.

Negotiations between the Palestinians and Israelis continued into the late 1990s and early 2000s at a number of locations, including the Wye River Plantation, Sharm el-Sheikh, Camp David, and Taba. At least four security issues were central to these negotiations.

First, Palestinian and Israeli negotiators discussed the possibility of stationing a U.S.-led international force in the Jordan Valley and on the Palestinian borders with Israel, Egypt, and Jordan. The December 2000 "Clinton Parameters" specifically argued that "the key" to establishing security "lies in an international presence that can only be withdrawn by the agreement of both sides" (Ross, 2004, p. 802). (See Appendix B.) Primary objectives of the proposed force would have been to monitor implementation of a peace agreement, prevent smuggling, and perhaps provide external security for the Palestinian state.[12] The force would overlap with a phased Israeli Defense Force (IDF) withdrawal from Palestinian territory. As several primary source accounts have indicated, however, there was substantial disagreement. Palestinian negotiators argued that an international force was necessary to ensure Palestinian security, especially in the absence of a Palestin-

---

[8] *Israeli-Palestinian Interim Agreement on the West Bank and the Gaza Strip* (1995), Article XII.

[9] Ibid., Article IX.

[10] Ibid., Article IX.

[11] *Treaty of Peace Between the State of Israel and the Hashemite Kingdom of Jordan* (1994). On counterterrorism and border crossing see Article 4; on criminal activity and drug trafficking, see Article 12 and Annex III, and on border crossing see Article 13.

[12] Ross (2004); Clinton (2001), p. 172; "The Moratinos Nonpaper on the Taba Negotiations" (2002), p. 88.

ian military. The Israeli government contended that an international force might be unresponsive to its security needs and complicate its right to redeploy in an emergency.[13]

Second, both sides continued to disagree about Israeli settlements—particularly such issues as the Israeli annexation of settlement blocs, contiguity between and among settlements in Palestinian territory, and further development of Israeli settlements in the West Bank. Palestinian negotiators pointed to the growth of settlements and rejected the creation of Israeli settlement blocs, which they viewed as a threat to the contiguity, security, and viability of a Palestinian state.[14]

Third, Israel consistently maintained that a future Palestinian state must be demilitarized and insisted that there should be restrictions on Palestinian weapons and military personnel. However, a Palestinian state would be permitted to have a strong security force for internal security purposes. Furthermore, Israeli negotiators requested early warning stations, mobile patrols, airspace rights, and supply bases in such regions as the Jordan Valley. They also required the right to redeploy forces to the Jordan River in the event of an external threat that constituted a "national state emergency" in Israel.[15]

Fourth, Jerusalem remained one of the most contentious security issues. Of particular importance were Palestinian and Israeli sovereignty rights over the Muslim, Christian, Armenian, and Jewish Quarters in the Old City; sovereignty over a number of holy sites in Jerusalem, such as the Haram al-Sharif/Temple Mount; and the city's status as capital of Israel and Palestine. Yet despite such differences, Israeli negotiators still agreed to cede significant portions of East Jerusalem to the Palestinians.[16]

Following the failure of Camp David II and subsequent negotiations to produce a breakthrough, the security situation rapidly deteriorated into a second intifada. Since 2001, there have been some discussions between Israelis and Palestinians. But security concerns have plagued efforts to end the conflict and create a Palestinian state. Following the death of Yasser Arafat, there have been additional steps toward easing security concerns. For example, the IDF handed over several West Bank towns, notably Jericho and Tulkarem, to Palestinian security control. The United States also sent special envoy Lieutenant General William Ward as "security coordinator" to assist Palestinian security forces and help coordinate Israel's disengagement from Gaza.

In sum, security has been—and will continue to be—the fundamental concern among Israelis and Palestinians. Despite some progress during the 1990s, the al-Aqsa intifada has served as a stark reminder of the tenuousness of peace and demonstrated the

---

[13] Report of the Sharm el-Sheikh Fact-Finding Committee (2001); Ross (2004); Ben Ami (2004).

[14] Ben Ami (2004); PLO Negotiating Team (2001), p. 156; "The Moratinos Nonpaper on the Taba Negotiations" (2002), pp. 81–83.

[15] Quandt (2001b), p. 32; Hanieh (2001), pp. 82–83, 93–94; "The Moratinos Nonpaper on the Taba Negotiations" (2002), pp. 87–89; Ross (2004); Ben Ami (2004).

[16] Ross (2004); "American Bridging Proposal" (2000); Malley and Agha (2001); Hanieh (2001), pp. 86–88, 95–96; PLO Negotiating Team (2001), p. 157; Ben Ami (2004).

need for viable security arrangements following the creation of a Palestinian state. Ending the Israeli-Palestinian conflict will require understanding security requirements for a settlement and embedding them in all aspects of negotiations. Both parties must openly and precisely agree about what "security" means, how it can and must be ensured during the onset of a genuine peace, and how security should be implemented over time.

Key Security Issues

The following pages discuss seven areas that we believe are central to external security concerns:[17]

- Border arrangements
- An international force
- Palestinian military forces
- Israeli settlements that may remain within a Palestinian state
- Intelligence, monitoring, enforcement, and dispute-resolution provisions
- Special security issues regarding Jerusalem
- The external environment as it affects Palestinian and Israeli security.

---

[17]In the discussions in each of these areas, some options may have little chance of being accepted by one or the other party. These options are included here to present a comprehensive picture of alternatives and arguments for and against them.

2. Border Arrangements

Ensuring Palestinian, Israeli, and regional security on a basis acceptable to both Israel and Palestine will require establishing workable border arrangements. Borders are a central issue in several respects: whether Israeli settlements will remain on the Palestinian side of the Green Line[1] separating Israel proper from the West Bank and if so—as, to some extent, is likely—what borders will be drawn in negotiations;[2] the design and nature of borders between Israel and Gaza following the withdrawal of some of the Israeli presence; whether there will be a special status for Jerusalem; whether both Israel and Palestine will have contiguous territory (perhaps involving land swaps); and how the West Bank and Gaza will be connected, e.g., either physically or "virtually"—i.e., by providing for uninhibited transit between the two areas.

The manner in which these issues are settled will depend on many factors, of which security is only one. As a general proposition, the more that territory is contiguous, that boundaries are clear and undisputed, that Israeli settlements are limited in the West Bank (in territories not ceded to Israel), and that Israelis and Palestinians can agree upon arrangements for passage of Palestinians between the West Bank and Gaza and other connections between the two, the easier it will likely be to solve security issues.

One critical dimension of border arrangements—the permeability of the border—does not necessarily depend on the resolution of matters raised above. Permeability is the ease with which people and goods will be able to move across Palestine's borders with Israel, Jordan, and Egypt—including passage between the West Bank and Gaza. The concept of permeable borders can include some limitations on the number of crossing points between Israel and Palestine, as opposed to "open" or "unrestricted" borders. There are at least three possibilities: (1) impermeable borders, especially between Israeli and Palestinian territory; (2) permeable borders without the presence of an international

---

[1] The so-called Green Line (formally the "Armistice Demarcation Lines") is the division between Israel and the West Bank that derived from the armistice agreements of 1949, especially that between Israel and Jordan of April 3, but which has no other juridical status.

[2] Most current proposals for Israel-Palestine peace presume that the Green Line will not be the final border between the two and that at least some Israeli settlements east of that line will be incorporated into Israel.

force; and (3) permeable Palestinian borders that are monitored with the assistance of an international force.[3]

Impermeable Borders

Impermeable borders would prevent most—if not all—goods and people from crossing the Palestine-Israel border, although exceptions might be made for government officials or other identified individuals. As Figure 1 illustrates, the current Israeli construction of a security barrier raises questions that are germane to this issue.[4]

Israel's work on the barrier, responses to it, and its effect on the negotiating process are beyond the formal purview of this study, which is devoted to analyzing requirements in the area of external security in order to promote a lasting peace and a successful Palestinian state. Our discussion of the security barrier focuses on what might be negotiated or done unilaterally by Israel in post-conflict circumstances,[5] noting that sovereign states have the right to determine the nature of security controls on their borders with neighboring countries. What happens between now and a potential peace agreement will be of significant importance, however. This will be especially true since, historically in the Arab-Israeli conflict, "facts on the ground," once created, have proved difficult to undo, with some notable exceptions—for example, Israel's withdrawal from Sinai under the Israeli-Egyptian Peace Treaty of 1979 and its withdrawal from Gaza in 2005.

The security barrier could affect many aspects of the creation and development of a Palestinian state, including the nature and conduct of its political, economic, and other relationships with Israel.[6] Some of these effects are discussed in detail in *Building a Successful Palestinian State.*

Basic arguments to be made for and against a barrier for the post-settlement period include the following.

---

[3] The degree of permeability is also a matter to be considered and negotiated.

[4] Devi (2003), p. 5; Lazaroff (2003); Bennet (2002). As with many other aspects of the Arab-Israeli conflict, the term used for the structures Israel has been building is subject for disagreement: Some refer to "wall," some to "fence"— and different parts might merit one or the other term. Here, the generic term "security barrier," as employed by Israel, which has been building it, will be used.

[5] Of course, events between now and the conclusion of a peace agreement—if it comes to pass—are important in helping determine the possibility of an agreement, the terms of negotiations, and the requirements for developing peace and security afterward. A barrier, once built, can also be torn down; but, as noted here, "facts" on the ground in the Middle East are rarely easy to change. Thus, psychologically, the creation of a security barrier, especially one that strayed from the Green Line or isolated Palestinian communities, could defeat a central tenet of the peace process: that there needs to be some significant degree of reconciliation and mutual acceptance if peace is to have a chance to be established. Given its sense of threat but desire for peace, Israel will have to make its calculations on this point.

[6] Lein (2002). Also see UNSCO (2002).

Figure 1
Security Fence Route Approved by the Israeli Government, February 20, 2005

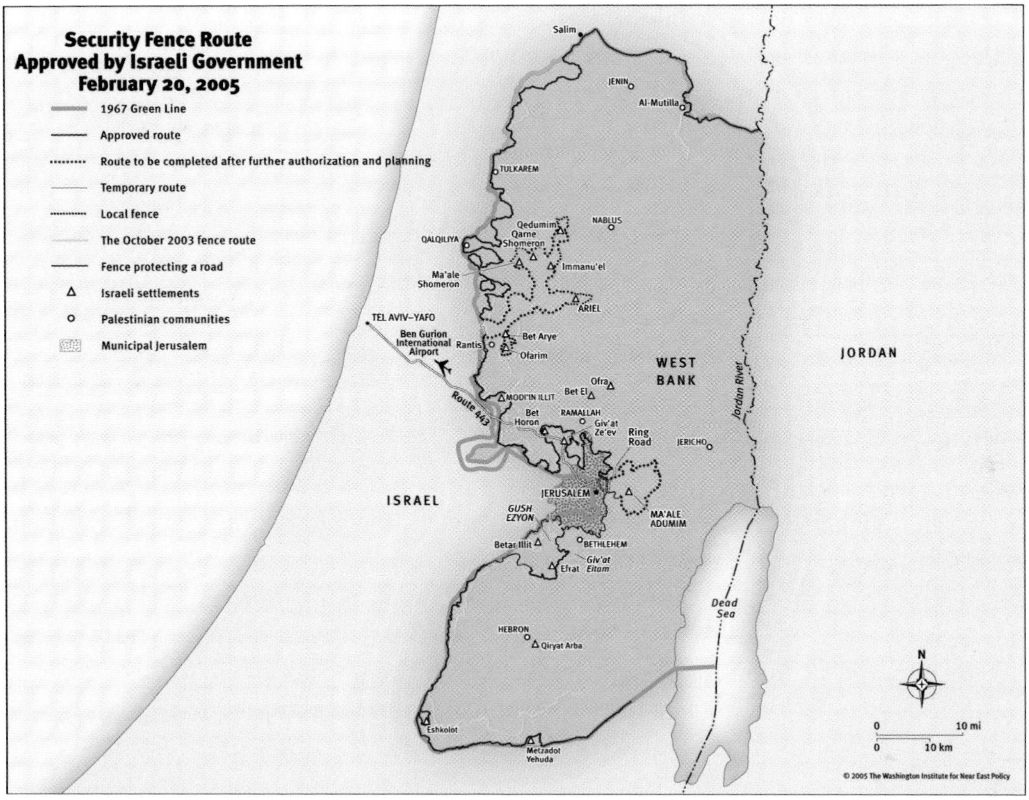

SOURCE: Used with permission from the Washington Institute for Near East Policy.
RAND *MG146/2-1*

Security Barrier—Arguments in Favor

Proponents of a security barrier, following peace, that separates Israel from Palestinian territory in the West Bank and Gaza argue that it would—and has—increased Israel's security by providing greater control over the access of Palestinians, especially potential suicide bombers, to Israel.[7] A barrier could help increase security between a Palestinian state and Israel for several reasons.

First, any physical barrier that decreased the ready flow of arms, insurgents, or terrorists into Israel would reduce the potential challenge to its security. This has certainly proved to be true in regard to a barrier constructed between Israel and Gaza.

Second, depending on how comprehensive the security barrier were following a peace agreement, it could decrease the costs of policing border crossings between Israel and Palestine, given that there would most likely be fewer checkpoints and immediate rear areas to

---

[7] Elizur (2003).

patrol than with a relatively open border. An international peace-enabling force[8] (discussed below) could also assist at checkpoints, as could joint Israeli-Palestinian units.

Third, a security barrier could decrease the opportunities for military action against Israel by organized units—e.g., attacks by guerrilla groups in Palestine or entering Palestine from abroad that managed to elude detection and eradication. Also, it could be made clear from the outset that the security barrier or portions of it would be of only limited duration—though perhaps measured in years—subject to the results of other peace-building activities.[9]

Fourth, by the same logic, a security barrier could support confidence-building measures—and perhaps be of value to Palestinians as well as to Israelis—by providing a greater sense of confidence about the borders between Israel and Palestine and limiting the capacity for parties who are unreconciled to peace to disrupt it.

Security Barrier—Arguments Against

Those who argue against a security barrier after a peace agreement suggest that it could have a deleterious effect on security. First, careful analysis would be required to determine how much a permanent security barrier—and of what kind—would increase Israel's security in the broadest sense, especially if Palestinians have no role, as is true now, in deciding its extent and degree of permeability. Further, although the physical barrier between Israel and Gaza has been highly effective, this might not prove to be true to the same degree along the extensive border between Israel proper and the West Bank.[10]

Second, a security barrier that continued after peace could affect aspects of the creation and development of a Palestinian state, including the nature and conduct of its political, economic, and other relationships with Israel. For example, a barrier that is substantial enough to protect Israeli security would also affect the economic viability of a Palestinian state, at least in the short run.[11] Thus, security considerations cannot be seen in a vacuum but need to be measured in relation to other factors.

---

[8] The term "peace-enabling force" is used here instead of "peacekeeping force" to indicate the broader range of issues for which the force could be responsible, compared with traditional efforts.

[9] These arguments presume that any security barrier remaining following a peace agreement would be along the line of the treaty-defined division between the two countries. The issues of the security barrier, its location, and matters related to it—including the manner in which people and goods could cross it—would no doubt have to be negotiated in any peace settlement. The definition of boundaries is likely to be complex, as seen in the demarcation of the Israel-Lebanon border after the withdrawal of Israeli forces in 2000, including adjustments made in some places of fractions of a meter.

[10] To some degree, the barrier could also inhibit Israeli retaliatory or preemptive military action because Israel would not have the same unrestricted ability to intervene in Palestinian territory as it has now. For Israel, that would be an argument against it; for the Palestinians it would be an argument in favor of it.

[11] Lein (2002). Also see UNSCO (2002).

Third, if a security barrier significantly reduced the capacity of Palestine to interact with the outside world, it could have a continuing, deleterious effect on Palestinian psychology—and undercut at least to some degree the effect of confidence-building measures between the two parties.

Fourth, a basic assumption underlying the peace process has been that an end to conflict is not enough. Rather, creating conditions to promote the development of peace "in the mind" (i.e., in the psychology of both Israelis and Palestinians) as opposed to simply "on the ground" (in terms of physical arrangements) is critical for the long term. Thus, some observers have argued that a highly obtrusive physical barrier separating Israel from Palestine would be inconsistent with a true two-state solution to the Israel-Palestine conflict. This effect might be reduced, however, if the barrier were clearly understood to be an interim measure, dependent on the development of other relations and confidence-building measures between Israel and Palestine.

Even if the Palestinians acquiesced in, or formally agreed to, whatever extent and type of security barrier Israel chose to maintain along the Israel-Palestine border, it would need to be permeable enough to allow sufficient throughput—persons, goods, and vehicles—in order to sustain a viable Palestinian economy.

Permeable Borders Without International Assistance

Another option is to have permeable borders, but without international assistance. This would involve establishing essentially permeable borders that are monitored by the respective governments with no additional involvement by outsiders. This was common practice for much of the 1990s before the al-Aqsa intifada. Individuals traveling across Israeli-Palestinian borders had to pass through both Palestinian and Israeli checkpoints for identification and inspection purposes.

However, there are several potential problems with this approach. At least in the initial period of Palestinian statehood, it is far from clear that there would be sufficient trust between Palestinians and Israelis to establish workable border arrangements without external involvement. There would need to be confidence that border guards and other security officials could perform their duties adequately. This border option would impose substantial requirements on the Palestinians for recruiting, training, and equipping border guards and security personnel, far beyond anything that has existed before. On both sides, there would also have to be a compatibility of methods, practices, and rules of engagement, to foster high confidence that these arrangements could be effective. We now turn to the most effective option: permeable borders with international assistance.

3. International Force

The best functional means for promoting security and mutual confidence would be stationing an international force along the Palestinian borders with Israel, Jordan, and Egypt as part of a peace settlement. This option has been discussed during the peace negotiations.[1] There are also partial precedents, notably the Multinational Force and Observers (MFO), which has been in the Sinai Desert since 1982 (see Appendix A and Table 1). But the circumstances surrounding the Egypt-Israel Peace Treaty are radically different from those that would occur under an Israel-Palestine agreement. The MFO is planted essentially in a desert; Israeli and Egyptian areas of strategic and military concern are widely separated; there are few civilians (and no Israelis) living within territory covered by the MFO's mandate; economic interaction (other than land transit between Israel and Egypt) is not at issue; and the MFO is not faced with a daily need to interact with Israeli and Egyptian officials under difficult circumstances or constantly to sort out complex and highly charged issues involving two mutually mistrustful societies.

An additional concern is that Israel has long been deeply wary of permitting its security to rest to any substantial degree in the hands of outsiders. Its experience with most European countries, including on matters of the peace process, has rarely been encouraging. Only the United States passes Israel's threshold of trust—and that view is not always shared by all members of Israeli society.

Characteristics of an International Peace-Enabling Force

In this subsection, we describe the preconditions of such a force; appropriate and effective leadership; agreed strategic, political, and operational objectives; clear and precise rules of engagement; and costs.

---

[1] On Israeli concerns about an international force, see the Report of the Sharm el-Sheikh Fact-Finding Committee (2000). On the possibility of an international force, see Quandt (2001b).

Table 1
Peacekeeping Missions in the Middle East, 1948–2003

Mission	Objectives	Peak Size of Military Force
UNTSO (1948–)	Monitor the cease-fire Supervise armistice agreements and demilitarized zones negotiated by Egypt, Lebanon, and Syria with Israel	572
UNEF I (1956–1967)	Occupy the buffer zone Oversee the withdrawal of forces from Egypt	6,073
UNEF II (1973–1979)	Establish a buffer zone between Egyptian and Israeli forces Supervise further measures of de-escalation	6,973
UNDOF (1974–)	Supervise the disengagement Patrol a 10-km buffer zone between Israeli and Syrian forces in the Golan Heights	1,331
UNIFIL (1978–)	Occupy the buffer zone Supervise IDF withdrawal from southern Lebanon Assist Lebanese government in reasserting sovereignty over the area	6,975
MFO (1982–)	Implement security arrangements after Israeli withdrawal from Sinai	2,500
MNF I (1982)	Oversee PLO withdrawal from Beirut	1,285
MNF II (1982–1984)	Provide an interposition force in the area of Beirut	5,500
TIPH (1994–)	Promote stability and security for Palestinians living in Hebron	160

NOTES: UNTSO: United Nations Truce Supervision Organization; UNEF: United Nations Emergency Force (I and II); UNDOF: United Nations Disengagement Observer Force; UNIFIL: United Nations Interim Force in Lebanon; MFO: Multilateral Force and Observers; MNF: Multinational Force (I and II); TIPH: Temporary International Presence in Hebron.

Preconditions

Our working assumption is that an external international force, of whatever nature, would be deployed only after peace is achieved.[2] In addition, in deference to the principle of sovereignty, an international peace-enabling force should be deployed only when asked for by the respective countries; it should disengage and depart if requested by both Israel and Palestine but not by only one of the parties.[3]

Other preconditions include the following:

- A legal framework acceptable to all parties, perhaps including a UN Security Council mandate (Chapter VI of the United Nations Charter)

---

[2] Although a case could be made for deploying an international force prior to peace, particularly as a means of helping to stop violence and to press the local parties toward agreement, that subject is beyond the scope of this study. It is also very unlikely that any outside states would be willing to engage in any such operation, or that it would be mutually acceptable to Israelis and Palestinians.

[3] A clear example of the risks of withdrawal of such a force was the decision by UN Secretary General U Thant to honor Egypt's request to remove the United Nations Emergency Force (UNEF) from the Sinai Desert in May 1967, thus helping to create conditions that prompted the Six-Day War. See Howard and Hunter (1967). See also Higgins (1969).

- Rules of engagement acceptable to all parties
- A mechanism for coordinating the activities of the international force with the other parties, including dispute resolution
- A leading role for the United States, which it is fully prepared to support, under circumstances that make this role acceptable to both Israel and Palestine—preferably within the context of a NATO or NATO-led operation.

Leadership

A leading role for the United States in any outside peace-enabling force would be indispensable, for several reasons. First, it is virtually inconceivable that Israel would accept delegation of its security, in whole or in part, to any external country or institution unless the United States were firmly engaged, committed, and in control of the external force—both juridically and practically. The United Nations would be unacceptable to Israel for a variety of reasons, including historical experience and lack of confidence in the ability of the UN to be a reliable security provider. However, a UN Security Council resolution would be instrumental in providing international legitimacy for any external mission, including one organized around a leading or exclusive role for the United States. For the participation of America's European allies in any peace-enabling force, including one developed within NATO, such a resolution would be indispensable.

Second, although the Palestinians would likely be more willing than Israel to accept a UN-mandated and even UN-led international peace-enabling force presence, they too should welcome a force led by the United States, especially because of the inhibiting effect that a U.S.-led force could have on any potential Israeli unilateral actions across the border into Palestine.

A third reason is that the United States has assumed principal responsibility for the development of a new security regime for the entire Middle East, including long-term U.S. commitment to its effective functioning. Following the 2003 war in Iraq, U.S. interests in the region are now inescapably tied to achieving this goal for as long as it takes, whether the United States acts largely on its own with a limited range of coalition partners or—as it is seeking to develop—in concert with other countries that also have vital interests in the region, notably European states.

This fact has been a major impetus behind renewed U.S. attention to Israeli-Palestinian peacemaking: The United States clearly cannot fulfill its other tasks and responsibilities in the region or secure its strategic objectives (1) so long as conflict between Israel and any of its neighbors continues, (2) until the legitimacy of Israel as a sovereign and permanent state in the Middle East is fully accepted by all regional governments, (3) until the Palestinians have an independent sovereign state, and (4) until the Arab-Israeli conflict is removed as an aid to terrorist recruitment efforts.

The undisputed position of the United States, in terms of its power in the region and its demonstrated willingness to deploy and use military force, gives it unique authority to help police an Israel-Palestine peace agreement. Although one could argue that U.S. credibility on Arab-Israeli issues with some parties in the Middle East has been severely taxed in recent years, achieving an Israeli-Palestine settlement would clearly accrue to the credit of the United States and should significantly enhance its stature in the region.

To be sure, engaging in an Israel-Palestine peace-enabling/peace-enhancing force would impose added burdens on the U.S. military. However—presuming that any U.S.-led international force would be introduced only after peace were achieved—the size of U.S. components and the components of other nations could be relatively limited, certainly in comparison with external forces currently required in both Afghanistan and Iraq, where a critical part of the militaries' role continues to be combat and pacification. Furthermore, peace between Israel and Palestine has been, for strategic reasons, high on the list of priorities for U.S. administrations. Thus, it is hard to believe that the United States would refuse engagement in some form of post-settlement international force if this were seen to be a significant factor in making peace both possible (a promise during the negotiating phase) and enduring (a reality in the peace implementation phase). This U.S. role could also be augmented by some form of participation by NATO allies (and others, as with the NATO-led Stabilization Force in Bosnia). It might be done through a formal NATO commitment under a UN Security Council mandate. It is almost certain that the U.S. Congress and American public opinion would prefer this option, in order to share the burden of such an engagement.

The possibility of such a NATO role has already been advanced in public. Thus, in visiting Israel in February 2005, NATO Secretary General Jaap de Hoop Scheffer said the following:

> Coming back to the peace process, clearly, nobody can predict its outcome. And we should not prejudge anything, including about the need for or the modalities of an outside support to a peace agreement. Furthermore, the responsibility for achieving peace and stability in the region lies first and foremost with the parties themselves. In that context and within these parameters, the idea of NATO assistance has been brought up.
>
> I have stated many times the necessary preconditions before envisaging any NATO contribution. There would first have to be a lasting peace agreement between Israelis and Palestinians. Moreover, the parties concerned must be in favour of a NATO role in its implementation; and there would have to be a UN mandate. These conditions do not yet exist. For the time being, NATO lends its political support to the efforts by the Quartet to realise the goals of the "Roadmap," which, again, should remain the immediate priority for the whole international community.[4]

---

[4] de Hoop Scheffer (2005). He made a similar statement to the Munich Conference on Security Policy on February 12, 2005 (online at www.securityconference.de/konferenzen/rede.php?menu_2005=&menu_konferenzen=&sprache=en&id=159&/, as of November 2005):

> I also believe that we should not shy away from already starting to think about a potential role for NATO in supporting a Middle East peace agreement. This is not a revolutionary idea.

Even if NATO (and others) were engaged, the U.S. role would still need to be considerable, perhaps dominant, as has been true in all military activities undertaken by NATO. U.S. challenges in establishing security and stability in Iraq following the 2003 war, as well as a good deal of anti-American sentiment in Palestinian territory and the Middle East more broadly, may also provide an impetus for involving allied countries in a peacekeeping operation.[5] Although some Europeans might prefer an external force to be led by the UN or even the European Union rather than by the United States or NATO, that is unrealistic for reasons presented above. NATO's involvement would also have the virtue of helping to ratify its role beyond Europe, providing a focus for NATO activity in relationship to the Alliance's 21st century agenda, demonstrating coherence and cooperation among allies on both sides of the Atlantic, and showing the American people that the Europeans were willing to assume shared military burdens. As Table 1 illustrates, international forces have been used on several occasions during the Arab-Israeli conflict, although their effectiveness has been mixed and the situation today is markedly different.[6] For instance, UNEF was deployed in 1956 along the Israeli-Egyptian border in the Suez Canal sector, the Armistice Demarcation Line in Gaza, and the international frontier in the Sinai Peninsula. Also, a UN interim force (UNIFIL) was deployed in southern Lebanon in 1978 to help increase security in the area, although it proved ineffective.

For years, politicians and academics have, at various times, highlighted the potential added value NATO might bring in supporting an eventual Israel-Palestine peace agreement.

But let me be clear: we are not yet at the point where an active NATO role is in the cards. There would first have to be a peace agreement between Israelis and Palestinians and a request from the parties for NATO to get involved, with the understanding that the prime responsibility for security should remain in the hands of the regional players themselves; and, I suppose there would be a UN mandate to support such a role. These conditions do not yet exist. But I believe that, if the call comes to NATO, this Alliance must be prepared to respond positively—and to play its full part.

It is no surprise that this idea is surfacing again. For reasons of military and political credibility, any multinational peace operation deployed to the region to support a peace agreement would likely have to include both North American and European forces.

NATO is the only organisation that engages North America and Europe both politically and militarily. It has the political and military structures necessary for the effective political management of peace support operations. It has long experience in the most difficult and complex multinational missions. It has the arrangements necessary to include contributions by non-NATO nations, and long practice at making it work. For all these reasons, there is a logic to a support role by NATO in fostering peace and stability in the Middle East region.

[5] See, for example, Pew Research Center for the People and the Press (2003), pp. 19–32.

[6] On the success of peacekeeping operations in the Middle East, see Diehl (1988).

Strategic and Political Objectives

An international peace-enabling force should have at least the following general strategic and political objectives:

- Help to establish a peaceful security environment by increasing transparency and trust among Israel, a nascent Palestinian state, and other relevant parties, such as Egypt and Jordan.
- Play a temporary and even-handed role in helping to create the conditions necessary for a peaceful and smooth transition to Palestinian statehood and to encourage Israelis, Palestinians, and others to establish the political will and capabilities to ensure peace on their own.

Operational Objectives

To accomplish these strategic and political objectives, an international peace-enabling force should have at least five operational objectives. In conjunction with Israel, Palestine, and perhaps Jordan and Egypt, such a force should do the following:

- Help to monitor and patrol border crossings, checkpoints, ports, waterways, airspace, and perhaps corridors linking the West Bank and Gaza.
- Verify compliance with the peace agreement.
- Join (where appropriate) in Israeli and Palestinian confidence-building measures and dispute-resolution mechanisms.
- Facilitate (where appropriate) liaison arrangements between Israeli and Palestinian security forces.
- Supervise population transfers of Israeli settlers and (if still pertinent) IDF from Palestinian territory, and provide security during this withdrawal process.

Help to Monitor and Patrol Border Crossings.   An international peace-enabling force could be stationed at checkpoints and along the borders to help Palestinian, Israeli, Jordanian, and Egyptian border guards inspect vehicles, individuals, and goods transported across the border. An international force might monitor these areas from static observation posts; traffic checkpoints; and mobile ground, air, and sea patrols, and report any violations.[7] However, this point would need to be considered carefully and negotiated precisely to ensure that the international force would be able to perform its assigned functions and avoid, to the degree possible, becoming a focus for opposition for any party (other than for external *agent provocateurs*, as may be unavoidable, at least in the early period of a peace agreement).[8] In addition, an international peace-enabling force could

---

[7] Hillen (1998), p. 51.

[8] Maintaining a position of "impartiality" while also being effective has bedeviled many peacekeeping operations. Thus, the U.S. Marines at the Beirut International Airport in 1983 came to be seen as favoring the Maronites as a

provide technical and financial aid to help the Palestinians and Israelis develop new or enhanced electronic surveillance equipment and techniques for use at borders, such as biometric-based personal identification and verification technology. Potential contributions in this area are discussed in the internal security chapter of *Building a Successful Palestinian State.*

Verify Compliance. The international peace-enabling force should also help monitor Palestinian and Israeli compliance with a peace agreement. This might include such tasks as overseeing the return of Palestinian refugees, if this were agreed upon in the peace settlement, and monitoring the specific aspects of agreement implementation, in particular, commitments to take action against terrorists and their organizations.

Join in Confidence-Building Measures. The international peace-enabling force should promote and supervise confidence-building steps, such as releasing prisoners and detainees, monitoring prisoner exchanges,[9] setting benchmarks for specific areas of cooperation, and developing practical situations of mutual trust among Israeli officials, police, paramilitaries, civilian officials, and others.

Facilitate Liaison Arrangements. Because it would be impossible to achieve any objectives without substantial information-sharing and coordination, the international peace-enabling force should act as liaison with military, police, and intelligence services from the relevant states. With both confidence building and liaison, the premium would be on devolving these responsibilities as soon as possible to the Israelis and Palestinians.

Supervise Population Transfers. Finally, following the outbreak of the al-Aqsa intifada in September 2000, the IDF over time reoccupied almost every major city in the West Bank. As the Oslo Accords provided, Israel currently has responsibility for the security of Israeli settlements in Palestinian territory. Consequently, a peace settlement that leads to the creation of a Palestinian state will mean that most—or all—Israeli forces will need to be withdrawn from Palestinian territory and redeployed elsewhere, as Israel has done with regard to Gaza.

Given that a peace agreement is likely to lead to a significant reduction in Israeli settlements in the West Bank, if not total withdrawal from all areas not incorporated in Israel—along with the withdrawal in 2005 of all settlements from Gaza—there will be relocation of Israeli settlers from Palestinian territory. An international peace-enabling force could supervise the redeployment of IDF units and population transfers, as UNEF I did following the 1956 war by monitoring the withdrawal of British and French forces

---

function of diplomatic activity. There was also the shelling of the Shuf Mountains. This transition from being perceived as "neutral" to *parti pris* was not sufficiently appreciated, a fact that contributed to the vulnerability of the Marine units to suicide attacks. By contrast, the restricted rules of engagement for the UN Protection Force (UN-PROFOR) in Bosnia did not permit UN units actually to protect civilians, with disastrous consequences, especially at Srebrenica in 1995.

[9] United Nations (1990), pp. 90–91.

from the Suez Canal region.[10] This means that an international force would monitor and inform relevant parties of the IDF's progress in redeploying and help ensure the safety and security of any Israelis who were relocating.[11]

Notably, there is as yet no serious suggestion that an external force should play a role in any of the functions discussed here in regard to the Israel-Gaza frontier following the Israeli withdrawal, beyond those European police already engaged on the Egypt-Gaza border. While that might be a logical "test case" of what is possible and a means for validating principles and practices of an external peace-enabling force, the caveats advanced by the NATO Secretary General (above) still seem to hold: Outside countries would not likely want to become engaged without there first being a peace agreement between Israel and a new Palestinian state, plus fulfillment of other conditions. And this would be true even if Israel and the Palestinian Authority wanted any such external peace-enabling force in regard to the development of the post-withdrawal situation between Israel and Gaza. Nevertheless, this is an issue worthy of further consideration and thorough debate.

Force Size and Capabilities

It is impossible to calculate accurately the size and precise capabilities of U.S. or U.S.-led peace-enabling forces that would be needed as part of a peace settlement, since these will depend on the specific mission objectives, the security environment in a Palestinian state, and other relevant factors. However, based on the objectives noted above and experience elsewhere, it seems reasonable to assume deployment of a total of between 2,500 and 7,000 peace-enabling forces (see Table 1). This presumes, of course, that the forces would not be permanently stationed everywhere within Palestine, but only where they would be needed on a regular basis (e.g., border crossings). They would also have a high degree of mobility, in order to move rapidly from a few central basing areas to where a crisis might arise. It is uncertain how long these troops would need to be deployed since this would be a function largely of the security environment and its evolution over time. It is useful to note, however, that no international force in the Middle East has been deployed for less than three years, and five operations are currently ongoing.

RAND identified at least 20 potential road crossings along Palestine's borders with its neighbors, Israel, Jordan, and Egypt. Assuming that there was a checkpoint at each— i.e., roughly 20 major checkpoints along Palestine's borders with these neighbors—a U.S. or U.S.-led force might require 20 platoon-sized units (approximately 40 soldiers each), for a total of 800 soldiers. These troops could assist the Palestinian security and border forces in inspecting vehicles, foot passengers, and material coming across borders, and be able

---

[10] On UNEF I, see United Nations (1990), pp. 43–78.

[11] During the Soviet withdrawal from Afghanistan, for example, the Soviet military informed the UN Good Offices Mission in Afghanistan and Pakistan (UNGOMAP) of all scheduled movements and changes of plans. It also supplied UNGOMAP with maps of withdrawal routes and detailed information on garrisons. See Hillen (1998), p. 53.

to respond with lethal force if attacked. Troops should be primarily equipped with light weapons, such as rifles and automatic weapons. Those at checkpoints with high throughput or that are located in high-threat locations could include tanks, armored personnel carriers (APCs), and helicopters for support—for both psychological and substantive value.[12]

The number and capabilities of international troops necessary would depend on at least three factors: the negotiated ratio of international to Palestinian forces, the rate of throughput at checkpoints, and the perceived security environment. The greater the percentage of effective, well-trained, and well-motivated Palestinian forces at borders, the fewer U.S. and other international forces would be needed. By contrast, the higher the throughput rate at checkpoints, the greater the number of troops likely to be needed. Finally, the more hostile the perceived security environment—either because of Israel's and Palestine's lack of confidence in one another or because of terrorist attacks or internecine Palestinian fighting—the greater the number of forces that would be needed.

For border and corridor patrol, the West Bank has a 404 km land border (307 km with Israel and 97 km with Jordan), and Gaza has a 62 km land border (11 km with Egypt and 51 km with Israel). A corridor linking the West Bank and Gaza would be roughly 30–50 km (60–100 km for two corridors), depending on where it is located. As examined in more detail in *The Arc: A Formal Structure for a Palestinian State* (Suisman et al., 2005), the corridor could include a comprehensive network of water, transportation, energy, and telecom systems. Based on the land borders of the West Bank, Gaza, and one corridor of 50 km between them, a wide range of forces could be required.[13] In general, the number of international troops needed would depend on the ratio of international to Palestinian forces and the security environment.

There are no clear parallels to provide guidance about the number of troops required. If the deployment of border and corridor forces were attempted based on the ratio of Indian forces per mile along the line of control with Pakistan, over 113,000 total troops would be necessary. But that is in a situation of active conflict where there is a possibility of war between two major powers. At more modest ratios, such as the U.S. presence along its border with Mexico or along the borders of its occupation zone in western Germany in 1946, approximately 1,600 and 6,700 total forces would be needed, respectively.[14]

---

[12] While circumstances of Israel-Palestine peace must be presumed to be radically different from those in Bosnia following the Dayton Accords of 1995, one lesson is, at least, worth exploring. The lead units of the American forces entering Bosnia as part of the NATO-led Implementation Force (IFOR) were deliberately "heavy" in terms of combat power, including the U.S. First Armored Division. The capacity of these units helped to catch everyone's attention and helped ensure that no shot was fired in anger.

[13] In the past, Israel has rejected deploying an international force to help monitor a corridor linking Gaza and the West Bank. However, we believe it should be considered by Palestinian and Israeli negotiators, and we have consequently included it in our assessment.

[14] The length of the India-Pakistan border is 491 miles, and there were 174,000 Indian forces (354 per mile) in 2001. The length of the U.S.-Mexican border is 1,951 miles, and there were 9,094 border police (5 per mile) in 2002. Fi-

Maritime and aerial surveillance would include aircraft and boats, supplemented by satellite reconnaissance. A squadron of coastal patrol boats might be required for patrolling, interdicting suspicious shipping, and monitoring vessels in Palestinian territorial waters, such as the Dead Sea and the Mediterranean Sea adjacent to Gaza. A monitoring unit of platoon size could be required at the Gaza seaport. At the Dead Sea, reconnaissance troops with radar capability and with several small assault boats for investigation and interdiction may be required.[15] Aerial surveillance would also be necessary at checkpoints, along the borders and the West Bank–Gaza corridor, and over bodies of water. Such surveillance might consist of several helicopters, unmanned aerial vehicles, Joint Surveillance Target Attack Radar Systems, other reconnaissance aircraft, and satellite surveillance.

These issues raise the matter of Palestine's control over its own airspace. Although this is important in terms of sovereignty, there would need to be clear understandings regarding the nature of air activity. One precedent is that of the four-power Berlin Air Traffic Control regime from 1945 onward, which not only kept commercial traffic relatively conflict free, but also managed some rules of the sky for the occupying powers, even during the Berlin Airlift. In the Palestine case, there is no need in the foreseeable future for an air force.

There would need to be at least one Quick Reaction Force (QRF)—perhaps one each for the West Bank and Gaza—with headquarters to provide fire support in case peace-enabling forces were attacked. These forces would have to be prepared to counter potential threats from suicide bombers, truck bombs, mines, rocket-propelled grenades, or sniper fire. The QRF might consist of several troop carriers, such as UH-60 Black Hawks, AH-64 Apaches, and perhaps some ground elements such as Humvees, APCs, and tanks. The total number of forces could range from a platoon (40 troops) to a company (150). In a more dangerous Palestinian security environment caused by an increase in terrorist attacks, Palestinian internecine violence, or Israeli-Palestinian tensions and lack of mutual confidence, the QRF might consist of a battalion or brigade and be appropriately equipped. A QRF should also include medical, intelligence, evaluation, force protection, engineering, and other support units. Depending on circumstances, a QRF could range from as few as 300 to as many as 5,000 troops. It would be an important component of the total force package, which we estimate could be between 2,500 and 7,000 troops.

There are a number of potential locations for airlift and sealift deployments. Airport options in Israel include Uvda in Eilat and Ben Gurion International Airport near Tel Aviv; in Egypt, Cairo International Airport and Sharm el-Sheikh Airport; in Jordan,

nally, the length of the U.S. zone's border in Germany in 1946 was 1,400 miles, and there were 30,000 border forces (21 per mile). *The Europa World Yearbook* (2002); Stacy (1984).

[15] See, for example, Canadian Department of Foreign Affairs and International Trade (2003).

Queen Alia International Airport, Aqaba International Airport, and Amman-Marka International Airport; and in Palestine if an airport of sufficient capability were constructed. Seaport options in Israel include Haifa, Ashkelon, and Eilat; in Egypt, Port Said; in Jordan, Aqaba; and in Palestine at appropriate points if suitable port facilities are constructed in Gaza.

Rules of Engagement (ROE)

A critical issue facing any international force is establishing the rules of engagement that tell a force, down to its individual members, what and what not to do in particular circumstances. Clarity and predictability are the essence, but so is the adoption of a set of rules that make sense for all concerned in the circumstances in which an international force is being deployed. ROE are particularly important in peacekeeping operations, where a high priority is placed on political as opposed to strictly military objectives and where there are likely to be few certainties, including who is the "enemy."

At least in theory, an international peace-enabling force should not be expected to assume responsibility for halting armed conflict between Israelis and Palestinians—or even among Palestinians—beyond situations that could be characterized as calling for police-type actions rather than the actions of combat soldiers. It is almost certain that few if any governments—including the United States and NATO allies—would be willing to take part in an international force unless they were assured to the extent possible that Israel and Palestine would not return to open conflict.[16]

This point may seem to beg the question of what an international peace-enabling force is designed to do. But it emphasizes the common understanding that any such force would be put in place only where there are willing local partners who primarily need political support, underpinned by a military presence, and assistance with making confidence-building and similar functions effective, while deterring and if need be countering internal provocations or external incursions. It would be difficult to recruit members of a peacemaking force in a potentially unstable environment, and this includes the willingness of the U.S. Congress to permit the engagement of U.S. forces. Furthermore, an international peace-enabling force cannot provide security for all of Israeli and Palestinian territory. Israel, for example, would not cede to anyone responsibility for its security against, say, military threats from Syria or from elsewhere. Indeed, the negotiation of an Israel-Palestine peace agreement presupposes efforts also to resolve the Arab-Israeli conflict in its entirety.

Nevertheless, an international force cannot assume that it is entering into a risk-free environment. Thus, the most difficult question for the United States and other participants in an international force would be how to respond if peace-enabling forces were subjected

---

[16] Since 1948 there have been at least five major wars—in 1948, 1956, 1967, 1973, and 1982—and substantial low-intensity conflict involving Israel, neighboring countries, and substate actors. Safran (1969); Smith (1996).

to attack from any quarter, beyond limited or random incidents. No matter how benign the environment might appear at first and no matter how much both Palestinians and Israelis want to keep the situation under control, peace-enabling forces must still calculate that they could face a variety of threats, ranging from suicide attacks to sniper fire, mines, and perhaps more intense challenges. In addition, the security environment in a Palestinian state that was being buffeted by internal tensions could conceivably deteriorate rapidly into civil war or Israeli-Palestinian violence.

Therefore, it would have to be clear at the outset that an international peace-enabling force would have the capacity and the powers for "force protection." This would put a high premium on several factors: the careful negotiation and establishment of rules of engagement, close liaison arrangements with Israeli and Palestinian authorities at all levels (political, intelligence, and operational), and a continued emphasis on confidence-building and fail-safe measures.

Such precautionary steps, clearly understood and agreed upon by all, would be a precondition for the stationing of an international force. Of course, these steps would also increase the reluctance of some outsiders to become involved.[17] The United States and others should enter "with their eyes wide open."[18]

Costs

Given the high strategic and political value of Israeli-Palestinian peace, cost will not be the determining factor in deciding whether to deploy U.S.-led peace-enabling forces to Palestinian territory. The United States and other contributing nations would have to consider whether deploying a force is worth the political, military, and other risks. If they judge that it is, they would likely be willing to pay costs even higher than those estimated here. However, policymakers may find it useful to consider cost estimates for planning purposes. While it is not possible, in advance of the precise details of a peace agreement, to accurately determine the full costs of the military components of a force (a bottom-up approach), it is reasonable to estimate the costs of a peace-enabling force in Palestinian territory based on the costs of the U.S. and NATO operation in Kosovo (a top-down approach). This estimate would be realistic since the Kosovo Force has had

---

[17] The NATO-led IFOR in Bosnia was effective, in part, because it arrived with heavy armor, a no-nonsense attitude, and large deployments. At the same time, the U.S. units were subject to disciplines not usual in combat forces to minimize the risks of casualties (force protection). Nevertheless, the sheer mass of the force, its broad composition in terms of nationalities, its potential for lethal action, its constant patrolling, and its combination with nonmilitary efforts certainly caught the attention of everyone in Bosnia, "friend" and "foe" of the peace accords alike. Circumstances would be significantly different in Israel and Palestine, but the point is still instructive.

[18] The MNF II in Lebanon, for example, engaged in combat with Lebanese substate actors and became involved in a civil war despite President Reagan's initial insistence, in a communication to Congress on September 28, 1982, that "our agreement with the government of Lebanon expressly rules out any combat responsibilities for U.S. forces." As an exchange of diplomatic notes in August 1982 stated: "the American force will not engage in combat. It may, however, exercise the right of self-defense." *U.S. Department of State Bulletin* (1982), p. 4.

somewhat similar objectives, scale, and equipment. Its primary task was to contribute to a secure environment in Kosovo by verifying the cessation of violence, patrolling territory, and overseeing the return of refugees and displaced persons. U.S. and NATO forces were outfitted with such equipment as APCs and tanks, similar to what we consider would be necessary for a peace-enabling force in Palestine.

Using U.S. Department of Defense data on the force size and cost of the Kosovo operation, we calculated the average per-soldier costs for military and civilian personnel, personnel support, operating support, and transportation.[19] We then used these numbers as a baseline for estimating the cost of peace-enabling forces in Palestinian territory. As explained earlier, depending on the precise terms of a peace agreement and the potential challenges to the peace at that time, between 2,500 and 7,000 forces could be needed to pursue such objectives as helping monitor and patrol Palestinian border crossings and waterways, verifying compliance with a Palestinian-Israeli peace agreement, and supervising population transfers. Consequently, based on the costs of the Kosovo operation, it is reasonable to expect that a peace-enabling force in Palestinian territory of between 2,500 and 7,000 soldiers would cost between $550 million and $1.5 billion per year.[20] As highlighted in Table 2, these costs include military and civilian personnel, personnel support, operating support, and transportation. All of these represent incremental costs—those that would not have occurred but for the operation.[21] Even much higher costs would be unlikely to forestall the creation of such a force if there were the possibility of peace.

In sum, contributing nations would have to calculate that the stakes for deploying a peace-enabling force were worth the political, psychological, military, and economic risks involved. But there should be no illusions about the potential for military engagement, and this should be clear to all. Indeed, the extent to which an international force were prepared for such engagement could signal the degree of its commitment to successfully underpinning peace.

---

[19] Force structure and cost estimates for Kosovo are U.S. Army estimates from the Office of the Secretary of Defense (FY2001 through FY2005). They include actual size and cost data for Kosovo from 1999 through 2003.

[20] We also estimated the cost of 2,500 and 7,000 forces in Palestinian territory using Department of Defense data on the force size and cost of the Bosnia operation. The data were from 1999 through 2003. The result was similar: $580.2 million for 2,500 forces, and $1.6 billion for 7,000 forces.

[21] For instance, the regular pay for active duty military personnel is not considered an incremental cost because it would have to be paid even if no military contingency arose. However, imminent danger pay only occurs during a military contingency, so the increase in pay due to imminent danger is considered an incremental cost.

Table 2
Per-Year Costs for a Palestinian Peace-Enabling Force (in millions of 2003 dollars)

Cost Category	Option 1: 2,500 Forces	Option 2: 7,000 Forces
Military personnel[a]	55.3	143.7
Civilian personnel[a]	6.1	17.1
Personnel support[b]	33.1	89.8
Operating support[c]	400.0	1,108.7
Transportation[d]	55.7	147.5
Total	$550.2	$1,506.8

[a] Military and civilian personnel include the incremental costs of deploying forces into the Palestinian theater of operations. Examples include hazard pay and costs associated with paying reserve personnel called to active duty.

[b] Personnel support includes food, water, equipment, and medical costs.

[c] Operating support includes the operation and maintenance of all forces involved in the Palestinian peace-enabling force. This comprises incremental costs for increasing flying hours; equipping and maintaining ground forces; buying equipment; maintaining command, control, and communications functions; and fixing or replacing damaged equipment.

[d] Transportation includes moving soldiers and equipment to the area of operations from bases in the United States and around the world.

4. Palestinian Military Forces

A key issue in the creation of a Palestinian state is whether it will be permitted to have military forces. As the term is traditionally used, it refers to forces that have the capacity for defense against potential external threats or other challenges, as opposed to border guards, police, intelligence services, or other essentially internal security forces. This issue is so important that neither the negotiation of a peace treaty nor the creation of an independent Palestine is likely to succeed unless a clear understanding and commitments are reached regarding the future of any Palestinian military forces. Our analysis suggests that a demilitarized Palestinian state with domestic security forces like police, rather than military forces, would be the most viable security option.

The principal external challenge to Palestine's security is the likelihood of externally fostered terrorism from elements that are unreconciled to its peace agreement with Israel. A second external challenge is the potential involvement of one or more of its neighbors in its internal affairs. Although the Palestinian Authority has maintained good relations with Egypt and Jordan, other governments could threaten the power of a Palestinian government, depending on the nature of the peace settlement and the makeup of the government. Syria and Iran, for example, have provided political, military, and financial support to organizations—such as Hamas, Palestinian Islamic Jihad, the Popular Front for the Liberation of Palestine, and Hezbollah—that have not always supported the Palestinian Authority's peace initiatives: indeed, some of which have actively opposed these initiatives.[1] Saudi Arabia has also supplied funding to some Palestinian organizations.[2]

It is conceivable that, if one or more of these neighbors became disaffected with a Palestinian government, they could attempt to destabilize or overthrow it through covert activity. Moreover, a peace settlement that resolved the status of the West Bank but not the Golan Heights may increase the likelihood of Syrian intervention, directly or indirectly. The possibility of such threats is a major reason for collateral efforts, by the United

---

[1] On Iranian and Syrian support for Palestinian groups, see U.S. Department of State (2003a), pp. 77, 81; Jane's Terrorism and Insurgency Centre; Levitt (2002, 2003).

[2] Mishal and Sela (2000), pp. 88, 162; Hroub (2000), pp. 165, 257; Jane's Terrorism and Insurgency Centre.

States and others, to secure broader peace and security in the Middle East, as discussed below.

In order to protect Palestine against these threats, a Palestinian military force might on the surface seem logical for a number of reasons, including issues of sovereignty, psychology, and prestige. There are few historical examples of sovereign states that have not had a military, at least to defend their homeland. It would be unusual to place restrictions on Palestine that are not imposed on any other country—at least not outside the context of voluntary and reciprocal arms control measures, such as those imposed for a limited period on the former German Democratic Republic after its unification with the Federal Republic.[3, 4] If the international community is prepared to support the establishment of a Palestinian state, its government could argue that it cannot be denied the inherent right of self-defense—although that argument must be weighed against other considerations.

However, the idea of creating Palestinian military forces poses significant problems. The challenge would be to structure a Palestinian military that met the actual or perceived needs of Palestine, including to counter externally mounted terrorism, without exacerbating the security concerns of other states, especially Israel.[5] This latter point is most important. From Israel's point of view, a peace settlement must mean not just Palestinian abandonment of the idea of eliminating the Jewish state but also the Palestinian state's controlling all activities in Palestine that could reasonably provoke an Israeli military venture against Palestine.

At the outset of an Israeli-Palestinian peace agreement, the viable option for a Palestinian state is to create effective domestic security forces, which may be able to counter externally mounted terrorism or threats from a neighboring Arab government.

Domestic Security Forces

The most logical option would be for a Palestinian state to have border guards, police, and other domestic security and intelligence forces—and not forces that would be, or could appear to be, regular military forces. In addition to general law enforcement and public order functions, the most significant threat to a newly formed Palestinian state may be from the inside and consist of challenges to the state's ability to gain and exercise a monopoly over coercive power—e.g., internecine struggles with armed Palestinian groups

---

[3] Countries that regained their independence from the Soviet Union or were created "new"—e.g., the Czech and Slovak Republics—remained bound by the limitations of the Treaty on Conventional Forces in Europe.

[4] As Palestinian Police Chief Ghazi Jabili has noted, "a state is not worth anything without an army that protects its civilians." Toameh (2000).

[5] The security dilemma literature is quite extensive. Some of the basic works include Herz (1950); Jervis (1978); Glaser (1994/95, 1997); Schweller (1996); and Kydd (1997).

competing for political power and externally based groups seeking to undermine the new state and its relations with Israel.

Small arms and light equipment should be sufficient for the Palestinian state to deal with such threats and challenges. Before the al-Aqsa intifada, the Palestinian Authority police and security forces possessed a range of anti-aircraft weapons, anti-tank weapons, small aircraft (such as transport helicopters), wheeled vehicles, and small arms such as pistols, rifles, machine guns, and grenade launchers. These weapons should be adequate for internal security purposes, although this need will ultimately depend on the capabilities of groups challenging the authority of the Palestinian state.

A further element of internal security will be for a nascent Palestinian government to maintain public order and to eliminate the capabilities and infrastructure of domestic groups that seek to attack Israel or to threaten the Palestinian state's legitimacy. Israel would have no reason to threaten Palestine's sovereignty—i.e., through military or "police" action across the border—as long as the Palestinian government can preserve domestic order and clamp down on groups that threaten Israel.

In time, an increasing range and degree of security responsibility in Palestine could be devolved to its government and its forces, depending on their proved competence and Israeli confidence. Over several years following the creation of a Palestinian state, it might be permitted, even under this option (domestic security forces), to create limited military forces beyond the parameters outlined here if they were judged to be valuable and important to a Palestinian state for legitimate security reasons. The issues involved would need to be considered at that time.

Palestinian Military Forces

An alternative option, which we believe would not be useful to support peace and security, would be to permit the establishment of Palestinian military forces along lines traditionally followed by other sovereign states in similar strategic or geopolitical situations.[6] But while this would not be advisable at the outset of Israeli-Palestinian peace—and would mostly likely impede Israeli agreement to a peace treaty—this option might be acceptable in later years, following the development of confidence between Israel and Palestine. Thus, this option is included here.

These forces could include some ground, naval, and air force units—but in any event these would not need to be large. Naval units could be designed to protect the coast against smugglers and terrorists. Because of geographic limits, a Palestinian air force would have little practical utility except for limited air defense. Most of our focus, therefore, is on the possibility of a Palestinian ground force.

---

[6] Luft (2001).

As noted earlier, the Oslo Accords limited the type of weapons Palestinian security forces could possess to small arms and equipment, such as rifles, pistols, machine guns, and wheeled armored vehicles. The process of creating a Palestinian army, however, might broaden this list to include such weapons and platforms as artillery, tanks, helicopters, mortars, and anti-tank guided weapons.

Weaponry and the capacity to use it pose two primary considerations. The first is what a Palestinian army might need for any realistic defensive purposes (essentially against third parties or—if internal security forces did not suffice—against externally mounted terrorism). The second is what weaponry and platforms the army would have that could be perceived by Israel, in particular, as both excessive to security requirements and potentially reducing Israel's or another neighbor's sense of security. Limitations on the forces would be needed. The following are some possibilities:

- Restrictions on the number and perhaps type of weapons and platforms, as well as on the size of the forces, their training, dispositions, deployments, and speed of redeployment
- Permanent liaison relationships with the IDF, including intelligence liaison and provision of support for training of forces
- A transparent relationship of military forces with Palestinian security forces, border guards, and police
- Clear and transparent civilian control of the military
- Limitations on mobilization and exercises
- External support for equipment and training from countries such as the United States, Egypt, and Jordan, as well as the European Union.

Within this framework, there are two basic options for Palestinian military forces at some point in the future. These options can also apply, at least in part, to Palestinian domestic security forces that would be created at the outset of peace.

Limited Palestinian Military Forces, with the Participation of Israeli Forces for Such Purposes As Exercises, Training, and Intelligence

This option could also include joint responsibility for Palestine's external security, especially along its borders with Jordan and Egypt, and in relation to internal security matters.[7] Major issues that would need to be resolved include organization, confidence- and security-building measures, rules of engagement, liaison and command arrangements, and dispute resolution mechanisms.

---

[7] The idea of Israeli forces deployed along the Jordan River, under circumstances where Israel would withdraw from most of the West Bank while annexing parts of it as well as parts of Gaza, became known as the Allon Plan of July 1967, because of its author, retired Lieutenant General Yigal Allon, who was then deputy prime minister and minister of Immigrant Absorption and who later served as Israel's foreign minister. See www.us-israel.org/jsource/History/allonplan.html and www.passia.org/palestine_facts/MAPS/1967-allon-plan.html.

An International Force Working with Palestinian Military Forces

This international force could be deployed in one or more configurations: along the Palestinian-Israeli borders, within both Palestine and Israel, on Palestine's borders with Jordan and Egypt, and presumably along Israel's border with Egypt. Several considerations would be involved, of which the following are most important:

- Israel and Palestine must both voluntarily agree to such arrangements and see them as making a positive contribution to mutual security.
- Agreed upon rules of engagement for the force would be needed, as well as agreements with regard to what it could and could not do and the range of its responsibilities.
- A lead role for the United States would be needed.
- Other states or international organizations, such as NATO, might be involved.
- Agreement on the source of authority (e.g., a UN Security Council resolution or an alternative) would be needed.
- This force would have to be linked to confidence-building measures and a dispute-resolution mechanism.
- An agreed upon term of mandate would be needed or at least criteria for judging security conditions that would have to be met before the international force could be withdrawn.

5. Israeli Settlements

Another major area relevant to external security is Israeli settlements. The issue of Israel's settlements has always been highly divisive. As illustrated in Figure 2, there are over 150 settlements in the West Bank that have been recognized by the Israeli Ministry of Interior, with a population of approximately 400,000. There are also dozens of outposts that have not been officially recognized.[1] While it is not possible to forecast precisely the terms of an Israeli-Palestinian peace agreement, it is likely that some Israeli settlements would remain in what is today Palestinian territory in the West Bank. However, if an agreement incorporated the concept either of land swaps and/or of ensuring the contiguity of territory, some or all of these settlements might be incorporated into Israel, without any interposed Palestinian lands. What follows is a discussion of alternatives if some Israeli settlements did remain within the compass of a Palestinian state, even though this possibility may be remote.

In past negotiations, Israel has demanded that it retain responsibility for security of both Israelis living in Palestinian territory and Israeli settlements located in Palestinian areas. For their part, Palestinians will seek to control all lands within their state, including jurisdiction over everyone living there.[2] Depending on how this complex issue is resolved—whether all at once or over a period of time—there could be significant implications for security, although these will be primarily about internal security within Palestine. However, if there were attacks on Israeli settlements within a Palestinian state (terrorist or other attacks), Israel would have strong incentives to respond militarily to incidents. In any case, the more settlements, the more complicated the security questions become.

---

[1] Foundation for Middle East Peace (2002). There are also roughly 33 Israeli settlements and 17,000 settlers in the Golan Heights.

[2] *Agreement on the Gaza Strip and the Jericho Area* (1994), Article VIII; *Israeli-Palestinian Interim Agreement on the West Bank and the Gaza Strip* (1995), Articles X and XII.

Figure 2
Israeli Settlements in the West Bank

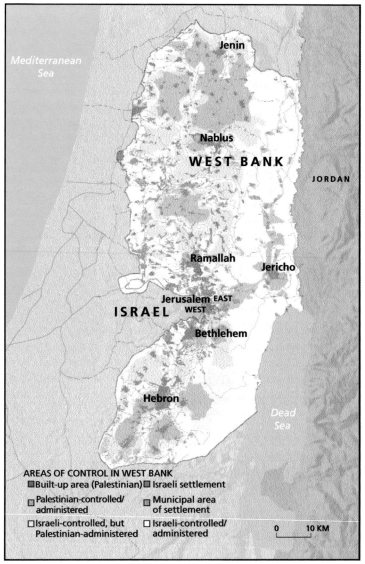

SOURCE: Map, B'Tselem—The Israeli Center for Human Rights in the
Occupied Territories at http://www.btselem.org. Copyright B'Tselem.
Overlays, *Newsweek*, November 22, 2004, p. 33. Copyright 2004
Newsweek. Reprinted with permission.

There are three general options for dealing with the issue of the settlements, all of which lead to the conclusion that for security reasons they should be minimized if not all withdrawn, except from areas incorporated in Israel, following creation of a Palestinian state:

1. *Israel would retain either sole authority or shared authority with the Palestinian government over any Israeli settlements that remained within the borders of a Palestinian state.* Joint authority might include Israeli-Palestinian policing arrangements, such as the establishment of Israeli bases and patrols in settlements, joint security coordination and cooperation committees for mutual security purposes, district coordination offices, joint patrols, and joint mobile units. Joint arrangements have been set up in the past for policing Palestinian territory.[3] This option would essentially be a variation of the status quo, since the IDF is currently the ultimate security guarantor of Israeli settlers. As Oslo II explicitly noted: "Israel shall continue to carry the responsibility for . . . overall security of Israelis and Settlements, for the purpose of safeguarding their internal security and public order, and will have all the powers to take the steps necessary to meet this responsibility."[4]

   However, this option is problematic. The existence of settlements in Palestinian territory has been a source of violent conflict since 1967. Virtually the entire international community—outside of Israel and the United States—believes that the settlements are illegal under such rubrics as the Fourth Geneva Convention, which states that an occupying power "shall not deport or transfer parts of its own civilian population into territories it occupies."[5] For their part, most settlers believe that Israel has legitimate and legal claims to the land, based on its historic and religious connection, as well as on the country's demographic and security needs. Unless all Israeli settlements were in areas incorporated into Israel and contiguous with its current territory, they are likely to be a target for rejectionist elements and conflict between Israelis and Palestinians within the borders of the newly formed Palestinian state, thus decreasing the security of both sides.[6]

---

[3] *Agreement on the Gaza Strip and the Jericho Area* (1994), Annex I; *Israeli-Palestinian Interim Agreement on the West Bank and the Gaza Strip* (1995), Annex I.

[4] *Israeli-Palestinian Interim Agreement on the West Bank and the Gaza Strip* (1995), Article XII.

[5] *The Fourth Geneva Convention,* Article 49, Paragraph 6. Consequently, individuals and terrorist organizations such as Hamas, the Palestinian Islamic Jihad, and the Popular Front for the Liberation of Palestine have attacked and killed settlers in both the West Bank and Gaza in an attempt to coerce remaining settlers into leaving. Israeli settlers have likewise attacked Palestinians and destroyed property such as homes and agricultural fields.

[6] Palestinian negotiators have resisted stationing any Israeli forces on Palestinian territory. As Yasser Arafat noted during the Camp David negotiations: "We will not allow the presence of any Israeli soldier on the border, in the Jordan Valley, or at the crossing points, all of which are sovereign Palestinian territory. The presence of any Israeli soldier there will render security invalid."

2. *Any Israeli settlements that remained in Palestinian territory would come under Palestinian authority.*[7] While some settlements, particularly those located near the Green Line, might be folded into Israel as part of a land swap in a peace agreement (as in the first option), the Palestinian government would have sovereignty over all communities, including Jewish settlements, located on its territory. In a final agreement, Israel might decide that Israeli settlers living in Palestinian territory would have to decide whether to relocate within Israel or live in settlements that are under Palestinian authority and patrolled by Palestinian police and security forces. However, this option is unlikely to be acceptable to Israel, and it will certainly not be acceptable to settlers.

3. *Responsibility for protecting Israeli settlements that remain in Palestinian territory would be given to an international peace-enabling force, either on its own or in cooperation with Palestinian police.*[8] Except perhaps as an interim measure during a phased withdrawal of Israeli settlements, this option is unlikely to be acceptable to the sponsors of an international force because it would require engaging troops in dealing with one of the most volatile points of conflict between Israelis and Palestinians.

---

[7] Israeli negotiators indicated in the January 2001 Taba negotiations that they may not need to maintain settlements in such areas as the Jordan Valley for security reasons, and in June 2003 Prime Minister Ariel Sharon stated that he supports the removal of at least some settlement outposts (although this may be for tactical purposes, related to so-called "illegal" settlements). Keinon (2003). On the Taba negotiations, see "The Moratinos Nonpaper on the Taba Negotiations" (2002), p. 82. However, this is contradicted by Israeli positions at the July 2000 Camp David negotiations. See Malley and Agha (2001), p. 62; Hanieh (2001), pp. 82, 93–94; Sontag (2001).

[8] Indeed, in the past, Palestinian negotiators have indicated that they could accept the stationing of U.S. or international troops in Palestinian territory in such areas as the Jordan Valley. See, for instance, Hanieh (2001), p. 94.

6. Intelligence, Monitoring, Enforcement, and Dispute-Resolution Provisions

In few other places in the world has the concept of political agreement and accommodation as an organic development been so important to the concepts of peace and security. This is a major reason that Arab-Israeli peace negotiations—even when in abeyance—have long been referred to as a *process*. Israel's proximity to Arab states has an unavoidable impact in terms of both the reality and perception of security—especially given the power of modern weaponry and the short distances between opposing military forces.

Thus, a critical factor in developing security has always been the extent to which Arab states and nonstate actors have come to accept Israel's permanent presence in the Middle East, both politically and psychologically. Treaties with Egypt and Jordan, as well as structured measures—such as formal dispute resolution commissions or outside "peace-keeping" observers and forces (e.g., in the Sinai)—are important, especially as transitional devices. But there has always been a sense that Israel's future can never truly be secure until its existence is no longer an issue. In a different but no less compelling manner, the acceptance of Palestinians as a people and their expression in statehood—in relation not just to Israel but also to other Middle East countries—is critical to lasting security, both in the immediate area and in the region. This is a reminder that the Arab-Israeli conflict and, certainly, the Israeli-Palestinian conflict have taken on symbolic significance.

As a result, security must be made up of many factors, only some of which relate to borders, forces (or the lack thereof), and other formal arrangements for military confidence. The process of developing relations between Israel and Palestine—and between both of them and other Middle East states—will be crucial, not just over the long run but also in the short term, to provide sufficient confidence to embark on the risky venture of peace. According to the theory that has always applied to Arab-Israeli peacemaking, old animosities and other alienating factors can in time give way to cooperation, however grudging, if perhaps not true friendship for generations to come.[1] This has been related to the so-called "bicycle theory" of Arab-Israeli peacemaking: the notion that it has to move forward, however slowly, or risk collapsing.[2]

The requirement is to find a way of creating a process of de-escalation and building momentum toward practical arrangements and developing trust. Cooperation and transparency between Israel and Palestine—perhaps including third parties—will thus be critical in a number of areas. In the security field, they include sharing intelligence information in a wide variety of areas: terrorist and criminal activities, verifying and monitoring that parties are living up to both the letter and spirit of all agreements, supervising the flow of legal weapons into the Palestinian state, inhibiting (if not completely preventing) the flow of illegal weapons into or through Palestine, and developing both formal and informal mechanisms to engage Israelis and Palestinians with one another, in part to help resolve the disputes and misunderstandings that will inevitably arise.

There are at least two basic approaches to such security cooperation:

- *Joint Palestinian-Israeli Arrangements with Little or No Third-Party Involvement.* Examples include intelligence cooperation and a variety of liaison arrangements, dispute-resolution mechanisms, and confidence-building measures. Such measures will be difficult to create, at least at first, because the al-Aqsa intifada eroded most of even the limited trust between the Palestinian Authority and Israeli government. Moreover, it is impractical to limit cooperation to only Israel and Palestine when a number of relevant issues—such as terrorism, criminal activity, and drug trafficking—have a broad regional or international scope.
- *International Involvement.* Given the difficulties of developing mutual trust from the outset, even in areas where confidence can eventually be built, third-party intervention can be beneficial and may even be a necessary condition for long-term cooperation between the two sides. The United States can play a particularly prominent role since it is the most powerful engaged country in the region and is trusted by both parties.

There are four general areas where U.S. and other international involvement could be beneficial.

---

[1] Thus, although the Egypt-Israel Peace Treaty of 1979 has led to what is often termed a "Cold Peace," there are few indications that Egyptians would be willing to see the conflict with Israel reignited.

[2] An example of the positive attributes of this theory was the sequence of negotiated agreements between Egypt and Israel that began at "Kilometer 101" in November 1973, west of the Suez Canal. The agreed upon disengagement was to gain its validity by the promise of the next step. The validity of the next step was to come from the step that followed, and so forth. At each step, earlier steps were "locked in" and, in effect, permanently accepted by both sides. Eventually, the final step was taken at Camp David and subsequent treaty negotiations in 1979.

- *Creation of joint intelligence committees* to promote intelligence cooperation between Israeli and Palestinian governments regarding such issues as the elimination of terrorist cells, the prevention of criminal activity, and reassurances regarding one another's military, political, and even economic activities and intentions.
- *Establishment of liaison committees to promote cooperation in areas of common interest*—such as security issues arising from the movement of refugees—among the governments of Israel, Palestine, and others in the region, such as Jordan and Egypt.
- *Dispute-resolution mechanisms and confidence-building measures.*[3] These will be crucial for dealing directly, forthrightly, regularly, and rapidly with inevitable difficulties, conflicts, differences of interpretation, and changes in circumstances. For example, if Israel demanded the right to redeploy forces to Palestinian territory in the event of a national state emergency, a dispute resolution mechanism would be critical for discussions between Palestinians, Israelis, an international force, and other parties. Indeed, in many ways, these mechanisms will be the linchpin of all security arrangements. The presence of outsiders, including an international peace-enabling force, will be helpful; but dispute resolution mechanisms are most effective when the responsibility rests squarely and exclusively on the two principal parties.
- *Provision of financial resources, especially for bolstering security efforts.* This matter would have to be balanced against other demands for money to create a viable Palestinian state. But given the stakes, this needs to be a high priority, if not the top priority.

---

[3] During the Cold War, the United States and the Soviet Union set up a number of bodies and mechanisms designed to help resolve disputes in areas where there was a mutual interest in doing so, despite the underlying conflict. Two such arrangements were Incidents at Sea, involving accidental encounters by naval vessels; and the Standing Consultative Commission created as part of SALT II to permit the United States and Soviet Union to discuss, in a structured and—in practice—nonconfrontational way, various concerns and discrepancies regarding the implementation of arms control agreements.

7. Special Security Issues Regarding Jerusalem

From the beginning of the Arab-Israeli conflict, the future of Jerusalem has been a major point of contention. Jerusalem is important to the three great monotheistic religions whose holy sites are located within a constricted, one-square-kilometer area in the Old City. And because of the presence of people of different religions, nationalities, and ethnicities, as well as overlapping claims to religious sites, it is hard to imagine a "clean," mutually agreed-upon solution that would leave critical parts of the city under the control of only one party. Part of the Israeli position since the 1967 war is that Jerusalem must be one city, undivided, if there is ever to be a true resolution of the various levels of conflict and contention.[1] An added complication in recent years has been the definition of the bounds of "Jerusalem," including the issue of Israeli settlements that are contiguous or nearby. In all, the status of Jerusalem has been one of the most contentious and complicated final-status issues; indeed, in the history of negotiations in the last several years, it has generally been seen as the last issue to be considered and resolved.[2]

Although it is difficult to predict how a peace settlement will resolve the status of Jerusalem, ensuring security will be a critical element of promoting peace and stability both in a Palestinian state and with Israel. The riots in the Old City following Ariel Sharon's visit to the Haram al-Sharif/Temple Mount in September 2000 illustrated the city's volatility. It is unlikely that a peace settlement will completely eradicate future unrest over the status of Jerusalem. The following discussion of options for Jerusalem focuses only on the security implications.

---

[1] The Israeli position continues to be that Jerusalem should be forever the capital of Israel. A critical issue, of course, is whether it can also be the capital of a Palestinian state.

[2] As Rashid Khalidi notes: "More than any other issue of the Palestinian-Israeli conflict, Jerusalem has deep resonance for all the parties. Certainly, there will be no end to the Palestinian-Israeli conflict, no Arab-Israeli reconciliation, and no normalization of the situation of Israel in the region without a lasting solution for Jerusalem." See Khalidi (2001), p. 82.

Palestinian Security Responsibilities in Some Sections of East Jerusalem

The Palestinian state would control security over all or parts of East Jerusalem, such as the Muslim and Christian Quarters of the Old City.[3] In terms of security,

- Demarking boundaries (hard or soft) would be critical.
- Liaison arrangements between Israel and Palestine would be necessary.
- An external presence (U.S. and perhaps others) would be useful, at least as a transitional arrangement. Whether this would be acceptable to either side would need to be tested in negotiations.
- Possible demilitarization of Jerusalem should be pursued, except for internal security forces, whether in single or joint responsibility, including joint security (police) patrols.
- Confidence-building measures, as well as dispute resolution mechanisms, could be organized through a unified or confederated municipal authority.

Israeli Security Responsibility in All of Jerusalem

This option would be a continuation of today's situation in practice. A variant might be to create an international committee that would give a Palestinian state custody over such areas as the Haram al-Sharif, but to allow Israel to have security control over the rest of Jerusalem. Or, to respect both Muslim and Jewish interests, the Haram al-Sharif (Temple Mount) could be put under joint custody of the two states or perhaps representatives of the two religions. This is the "custodial sovereignty" versus "residual sovereignty" arrangement that was debated at the 2000 Camp David summit.[4] Another option is to give Israel sovereignty and control over security in Jerusalem and to establish Abu Dis as a substitute Palestinian capital. The security implications of this option would be the simplest in terms of the technical capacity of Israel to exercise authority, but it has been rejected by Palestinian leaders in the past, and there is no sign that it will be acceptable in the future.

---

[3] Palestinian leaders have indicated that any peace settlement must give them sovereignty over all or part of East Jerusalem (which they consider their capital), including a number of neighborhoods outside the walls of the Old City such as Musrara, Shaykh Jarrah, Salah al-Din, Suwwana, Wadi al-Juz, Silwan, and Ras al-Amud. During the Camp David negotiations, Arafat was quoted as saying: "The Palestinian leader who will give up Jerusalem has not yet been born. I will not betray my people or the trust they have placed in me." Hanieh (2001), p. 85. It appears that Palestinian and Israeli negotiators might agree in principle to the Clinton suggestion of Palestinian sovereignty over Arab neighborhoods in East Jerusalem and Israeli sovereignty over Jewish neighborhoods. "The Moratinos Nonpaper on the Taba Negotiations" (2002), p. 83; Malley and Agha (2001), p. 62.

[4] Hanieh (2001), pp. 83–84.

International Security Responsibility in Jerusalem (or Sections Thereof)

A third option would be for the United Nations—or some other internationally sanctioned body—to be given security control over the Old City and environs of Jerusalem or sections thereof. One alternative would be to give a mutually accepted international force authority over all sacred sites in both East and West Jerusalem.[5] Temporary international security control over the Haram al-Sharif/Temple Mount has also been discussed for a specified period, after which the parties would either agree on a new solution or extend the existing arrangements.[6] The nature of overall security relations between Israel and the Palestinian state would be key.

---

[5] Khalidi (2001), p. 86.

[6] "The Moratinos Nonpaper on the Taba Negotiations" (2002), p. 85.

8. External Security Environment

Finally, we turn to the external security environment. In few places in the world does the potential for security between two states—in this case Israel and Palestine—depend so much on the external environment. The most desirable outcome, of course, is peace and security throughout the region. But given the current and likely future state of the Middle East, that outcome is unlikely for at least the foreseeable future. Following war in Iraq, the United States (along with its allies) has acquired major responsibilities for the region—for a generation and perhaps beyond—and U.S. credibility is very much at stake. It must follow through on its obligations, however long is necessary, and this will be true—in some deeply engaging form—whatever happens in the near future in Iraq, in regard to U.S. and other coalition forces there; in regard to challenges relating to Syria, Iran, Saudi Arabia, and other countries; and about the ongoing war on terrorism. Clearly, this background will deeply influence the development of security arrangements between Israel and the Palestinian state, as well as the value of and requirement for outside security engagement.

The Situation of External States with Regard to Israel

A Comprehensive Peace Settlement

If an Israeli-Palestinian peace agreement and the creation of a Palestinian state were achieved in parallel with the conclusion of other agreements with Israel—especially by Syria but also by Lebanon—then the prospects for success of the new peace agreement would be enhanced. Recent ferment involving both countries has increased interest in this possibility. Prospects for success would be enhanced still further if there were genuine reconciliation of other Arab states to both the peace agreement and Israel's place within the region. Such agreements would have significant implications for security, at least in the medium to long term, with regard to the arrangements for external security of the Palestinian state (its borders with Jordan and Egypt), the potential size and character of any Palestinian military forces, the type and pace of confidence-building measures, and the value and role of an international force. In this variant, these security requirements would be more modest than otherwise. However, the negotiation of an Israeli-Palestinian peace agreement may take place before external relationships and attitudes become clear.

A Limited Peace Settlement

If an Israeli-Palestinian peace agreement has to stand by itself—or if there are still significant Arab states unreconciled to the agreement or even to Israel's existence—then the security requirements for the new Palestinian state, along with Israeli concerns, will be greater. This would increase both the value of an international military force (led by the United States) and Israeli requirements for a role in the Palestinian state's external security—e.g., along the Jordan River and on the borders with Egypt. As a result, Israel, Palestine, states like Jordan and Egypt, and outside backers—beginning with the United States—have a strong incentive to place this diplomacy in the broader context of the Middle East.

The Degree of Stability in the Middle East

What happens in the Middle East as a whole is thus a critical factor in determining the security requirements for a new Palestinian state. Other developments in the Middle East are related to the overall sense of confidence that Israeli-Palestinian relations can be isolated (to the degree possible) from broader, security-challenging events. They are also related to the responsibilities that the United States has now assumed to help provide an overall structure of regional stability[1] and to the extent to which the sources of support for regionally based terrorism and anti-Israeli activity are either increased or decreased. Obviously, the more effective external diplomacy and other stability-enhancing efforts are—including the major undertaking the United States is now embarked upon in Iraq—the lower the security requirements and the more likely that Israel and Palestine can arrive at workable arrangements. There are two important considerations: externally mounted terrorism and developments in key regional countries.

The amount and seriousness of terrorism from outside that is directed against either Palestine, Israel, or an international peace force will depend in large part on the degree of

---

[1] In time, security in the Middle East could be advanced by the creation of some new form of security structure for the region as a whole, or at least major parts of the region. There are few if any precedents in terms of form—the defunct Central Treaty Organization (CENTO) may have come the closest. But the collapse of the "old order" clearly demands some new organizing principles, especially if the United States, perhaps with other Western states, is not to have to assume security responsibilities for the region for the indefinite future. If there were such a new regional security structure, both Israel and Palestine should be part of it.

stability in the region as a whole and the extent to which Israel (as an entity) or any Israeli actions continue to be symbols or rallying points for terrorists. To help recruit a new generation of supporters, terrorists have cited what they argue to be a lack of U.S. evenhandedness in the Arab-Israeli peace process, Israel's Western orientation, and whatever else the United States is doing in the region and beyond. If the United States follows through on its declared intentions for post-conflict Iraq in terms of politics and resources and if the U.S. administration perseveres in its bold initiatives in promoting Israeli-Palestinian negotiations, there is likely to be less of a challenge from external terrorism directed at the peace process, Israel, or Palestinians characterized as collaborators. The exception, of course, will be rejectionist elements such as al-Qaeda. There is also a history of increased terrorism when the peace process seems ready to make a breakthrough.

Another key variable is what is happening in other countries in the region—such as Iran, Saudi Arabia, Syria, and Egypt—that would either reduce the threat of terrorism or develop in such a way that terrorism or some other threat of outside intervention increases. In the medium term, the degree of terrorism focused on the Palestinian-Israeli space will turn in part on the degree to which Israel and Palestine demonstrate genuine reconciliation, cooperation, and major successes in development and living conditions for the Palestinian people: Economic and political efforts *after* peace can contribute to reconciliation, whereas *before* peace they are unlikely to have that effect.

Arab-Israeli peacemaking has always been plagued by elements in both Arab and Israeli society that have not supported the goals or the process of peacemaking. Extremists on both sides have, at times, made implicit common cause. One function of the Israeli-Palestinian peace process is to create conditions, goals, and processes that will sideline skeptics and opponents of peace.

9. Conclusion

At the time of this writing, the prospects for reviving a viable peace process between Israel and the Palestinians have reached a level not seen for several years. The Quartet countries have rededicated themselves to pursuit of the Roadmap. U.S.-European relations, including over Middle East issues, have improved from the nadir reached at the time of the Iraq War. While U.S. attention, which is crucial for forward movement, is still turned largely toward continuing conflict in Afghanistan and Iraq, the administration has committed itself to pursuit of Israeli-Palestinian peace. Following the death of Yasser Arafat, successful presidential elections in the Palestinian territories, Israel's withdrawal from Gaza, and a general decrease in violence between Israelis and Palestinians, there are opportunities for peacemaking.

As we have discussed here, security may be only one factor in determining whether there will be peace between Israel and a new state of Palestine and whether such a state will be successful—a quality defined in significant part in terms of the political and strategic relationship that the two states have with one another. But security is most important among indispensable factors—security both internal to the Palestinian state and external to it and to Israel. At the same time, all must recognize that external security for the Palestinian-Israeli space will need to be a compound of many factors. Several have been discussed here. Some will be the subject of negotiations in the process of creating peace, while options for others will only be dealt with after a peace agreement. All will have substantial effects on the external security environment of the new state. These options must also be seen in full relationship to every other aspect of creating a Palestinian state, its relations with Israel, its role in the Middle East and beyond, and the various processes that can, in time, enable Palestinians and Israelis to build their respective free, independent, sovereign, and democratic societies together, to common ends.

This remains the central challenge of building peace between Israel and its neighbors, and of providing the basis for a viable Palestinian state. "Security"—both external and internal—is not the be-all and end-all. But without it, to a degree matched by few other places in the world, nothing else constructive is possible. Security first; the rest can follow.

Security Issues and the Arab-Israeli Peace Process, 1967–2003

Agreement/Proposal	Date	International Security Issues	Palestinian Domestic Security Issues
UN Security Council Resolution (UNSCR) 242	Nov. 22, 1967	Withdraw Israeli armed forces from territories occupied in 1967 war	
UNSCR 338	Oct. 22, 1973	Stop fighting and terminate all military activity immediately Implement UNSCR 242	
UNSCR 425	March 19, 1978	Cease Israeli military action against Lebanese territorial integrity and withdraw forces from all Lebanese territory Establish UN interim force for southern Lebanon	
Camp David Accord	Sept. 17, 1978	Permit full exercise of Egyptian sovereignty up to the internationally recognized border between Egypt and mandated Palestine Withdraw Israeli forces from the Sinai Establish right of free passage of ships through Gulf of Suez and Suez Canal Include participation of Israeli and Jordanian forces in joint patrols Station UN forces in (a) the Sinai and (b) the Sharm el-Sheik area to ensure freedom of passage through the Straight of Tiran	Establish a strong local police force in the West Bank and Gaza, which may include Jordanian citizens Police will maintain liaison on internal security matters with designated Israeli, Jordanian, and Egyptian officers
Peace Treaty Between Israel and Egypt	March 26, 1979	End state of war between Israel and Egypt Withdraw Israeli armed forces and civilians from the Sinai Station UN personnel who will help operate check-points, reconnaissance patrols, and observation posts along the interim buffer zone Establish a Joint Commission to facilitate implementation of the treaty Continue U.S. airborne surveillance flights until the completion of the final Israeli withdrawal	Egypt and Israel may establish and operate early warning systems in certain zones

Agreement/Proposal	Date	International Security Issues	Palestinian Domestic Security Issues
Memorandum of Understanding between the United States and Israel	Nov. 30, 1981	Agree to enhance strategic cooperation to deter all threats from the Soviet Union in the region Hold joint military exercises and readiness activities Agree to military cooperation	
Israeli Peace Initiative	May 14, 1989		Accord self-rule to inhabitants of Judea, Samaria, and Gaza Propose free and democratic elections among the Palestinian Arab inhabitants of Judea, Samaria, and the Gaza district Israel will continue to be responsible for security, foreign affairs, and all matters concerning Israeli citizens Israel opposes the establishment of an additional Palestinian state in the Gaza district and in the area between Israel and Jordan Israel will not conduct negotiations with the PLO
Israel-PLO recognition—exchange of letters between Yitzhak Rabin and Yasser Arafat	Sept. 1993	PLO recognizes Israel to exist in peace and security PLO accepts UNSCRs 242 and 338 PLO renounces use of terrorism and other acts of violence Israel recognizes PLO as the representative of the Palestinian people	

Agreement/Proposal	Date	International Security Issues	Palestinian Domestic Security Issues
Oslo I—Declaration of Principles on Interim Self-Government Arrangements	Sept. 13, 1993	Redeploy Israeli forces in the West Bank and Gaza Israel will continue to have authority over external security, settlements, Israelis, and foreign relations Establish a Joint Israeli-Palestinian Liaison Committee to deal with a number of issues—including security issues Establish a temporary international or foreign presence Invite Jordan and Egypt to participate in establishing further liaison and cooperation arrangements	Establish strong police force in order to guarantee public order and internal security for the Palestinians of the West Bank and Gaza Recruit police officers locally and from abroad holding Jordanian passports and Palestinian documents issued by Egypt Israeli military forces and civilians may continue to use roads freely within Gaza and the Jericho area
Israel-Jordan Common Agenda	Sept. 14, 1993	Agree not to threaten each other by any use of force	

Agreement/Proposal	Date	International Security Issues	Palestinian Domestic Security Issues
Israel-PLO agreement on Gaza and the Jericho area	May 4, 1994	Functional jurisdiction of the Palestinian Authority (PA) does not include foreign relations, external security, international security PA will not have powers in the sphere of foreign relations. This includes the establishment of embassies, consulates, or other types of foreign missions; the appointment or admission of diplomatic and consular staff; and the exercise of diplomatic functions Israel and PA agree to abstain from incitement—including hostile propaganda—against each other Invite Jordan and Egypt to participate in establishing liaison and cooperation arrangements between Israel and PA Agree to a temporary international or foreign presence in Gaza and the Jericho area Establish joint security coordination and cooperation committees for mutual security purposes, district coordination offices, joint patrols, and joint mobile units	Establish a strong PA police force—the Palestinian Directorate of Police Force—that is responsible for: 1. Performing normal police functions, including maintaining internal security and public order 2. Protecting the public and its property 3. Adopting all measures necessary for preventing crime in accordance with the law 4. Protecting public installations and places of special importance Police force shall be composed of four branches: 1. Civil Police (Al Shurta) 2. Public Security 3. Intelligence 4. Emergency Services and Rescue (Al Difa'a Al Madani) Establish a Palestinian Coastal Police Limit police to 9,000 policemen Both sides shall agree to the list of Palestinians recruited Restrict police arms, ammunition and equipment, and related matters to: 7,000 light personal weapons Up to 120 machine guns of 0.3" or 0.5" caliber Up to 45 wheeled armored vehicles Communication systems Distinctive uniforms Jurisdiction of PA does not include the public order of settlements, the Military Installation Area, or Israelis Except for the Palestinian Police, no other armed force shall be established or operate in Gaza or the Jericho area
Washington Declaration	July 25, 1994	End the state of belligerency between Jordan and Israel	

Agreement/Proposal	Date	International Security Issues	Palestinian Domestic Security Issues
Israel-PLO Agreement on Preparatory Transfer of Powers and Responsibilities	Aug. 29, 1994		PA may bring disciplinary proceedings concerning persons it employs in the West Bank before disciplinary tribunals operating in Gaza or the Jericho area PA may authorize employees to act as civilian inspectors to monitor compliance with laws and regulations within spheres of education and culture, health, social welfare, tourism, and taxation. However, these inspectors shall not wear uniforms or carry arms, and they shall not in any other way have the nature of a police force
Israel-Jordan Peace Treaty	Oct. 26, 1994	Establish peace between Israel and Jordan Recognize the international boundary and each other's territory, territorial waters, and airspace as inviolable Cooperate on combating crime and drugs—exchange of information and transmission of evidence Establish procedures for border crossing	
Oslo II—Israeli-Palestinian Interim Agreement on the West Bank and the Gaza Strip	Sept. 28, 1995	Israel shall continue to carry the responsibility for external security, as well as the responsibility for overall security of Israelis Israel shall continue to carry the responsibility for protecting the Egyptian and Jordanian borders PA will not have powers and responsibilities in the sphere of foreign relations—including the establishment abroad of embassies, consulates, or other types of missions. The PLO may conduct negotiations for the following issues: 1. Economic agreements 2. Agreements with donor countries for the provision of assistance to the PA 3. Agreements for the purpose of regional development plans 4. Cultural, scientific, and educational agreements	PA shall have an independent judicial system composed of independent Palestinian courts and tribunals PA shall establish a strong police force that shall be responsible for handling public order incidents in which only Palestinians are involved Duties and functions of Palestinian Police include: 1. Maintaining internal security and public order 2. Protecting the public and all other persons present in the areas, as well as protecting their property 3. Adopting all measures necessary for preventing crime in accordance with the law 4. Protecting public installations, infrastructure, and places of special importance 5. Preventing acts of harassment and retribution 6. Combating terrorism and violence, and preventing incitement to violence

Agreement/Proposal	Date	International Security Issues	Palestinian Domestic Security Issues
Oslo II—Israeli-Palestinian Interim Agreement on the West Bank and the Gaza Strip (continued)	Sept. 28, 1995	Redeployment of Israeli military forces Establishment of Palestinian-Israeli joint security coordination and cooperation committees for mutual security purposes, regional security committees, district coordination offices, joint patrols, and joint mobile units	Palestinian Police shall consist of six branches: 1. Civil Police (Al Shurta) 2. Public Security 3. Preventive Security 4. Amn Al Ri'asah 5. Intelligence 6. Emergency Services and Rescue (Al Difa'a Al Madani) Total number of policemen cannot exceed 30,000 Establish Palestinian Coastal Police Terminate immediately the employment of policemen who have been convicted of serious crimes, or have been found to be actively involved in terrorist activities subsequent to their recruitment In the West Bank, the Palestinian Police will possess the following arms and equipment: Up to 4,000 rifles Up to 4,000 pistols Up to 120 machine guns of 0.3" or 0.5" caliber Up to 15 light, unarmed riot vehicles In Gaza, the Palestinian Police will possess the following arms and equipment: 7,000 light personal weapons Up to 120 machine guns of 0.3" or 0.5" caliber Up to 45 wheeled armored vehicles Rachel's Tomb will be under the security responsibility of Israel Palestinian police and Israeli military forces will conduct joint security activities on the main roads Palestinian Police will notify West Bank joint regional security committees of the names of policemen, the numbers on plates of police vehicles, and serial numbers of weapons Palestinian Police will act systematically against all expressions of violence and terror Create safe passage connecting the West Bank and Gaza Israelis shall under no circumstances be apprehended or placed in custody or prison by Palestinian authorities. However, Israeli suspects may be detained in place

Agreement/Proposal	Date	International Security Issues	Palestinian Domestic Security Issues
Sharm el-Sheikh Final Statement of Peacemakers	March 13, 1996	Egypt and United States declare support for the Israel-Palestinian peace process	
Israel-Lebanon Ceasefire Understanding	April 26, 1996	Establish a monitoring group consisting of the United States, France, Syria, Lebanon, and Israel Affirm that: 1. Armed groups in Lebanon will not carry out attacks by Katyusha rockets or by any kind of weapons into Israel 2. Israel and those cooperating with it will not fire any kind of weapon at civilian targets in Lebanon	
Agreement on Temporary International Presence in the City of Hebron	May 9, 1996	Establish temporary international presence in the city of Hebron (TIPH) to assist in promoting stability and in monitoring and reporting the efforts to maintain normal life in Hebron	
Protocol Concerning the Redeployment in Hebron	Jan. 17, 1997		The Palestinian Police will assume responsibility in Area H-1 following Israeli redeployment Israel will retain all powers and responsibilities for internal security and public order in Area H-2 Israel will continue to carry the responsibility for overall security of Israelis The Palestinian Police will be responsible for the following Jewish Holy Sites: The Cave of Othniel Ben Knaz (El-Khalil); Elonei Mamre (Haram Er-Rameh); Eshel Avraham (Balotat Ibrahim); and Maayan Sarah (Ein Sarah)

Agreement/Proposal	Date	International Security Issues	Palestinian Domestic Security Issues
Wye River Memorandum	Oct. 23, 1998	Create a U.S.-Palestinian committee to review steps being taken to eliminate terrorist cells and the support structure that plans, finances, supplies, and abets terror Establish a U.S.-Palestinian-Israeli committee to assist and enhance cooperation in preventing the smuggling or other unauthorized introduction of weapons or explosive materials into areas under Palestinian jurisdiction A U.S.-Palestinian-Israeli committee will meet on a regular basis to monitor cases of possible incitement to violence or terror and to make recommendations and reports on how to prevent such incitement	PA agrees to take all measures necessary in order to prevent acts of terrorism, crime, and hostilities directed against the Israeli side, against individuals falling under the Israeli side's authority, and against their property Establish several security actions: 1. Outlawing and combating terrorist organizations 2. Prohibiting illegal weapons 3. Preventing incitement The Palestinian side will provide a list of its policemen to the Israeli side
Sharm el-Sheikh Memorandum	Sept. 4, 1999		PA and Israel agree to ensure the immediate, efficient, and effective handling of any incident involving a threat or act of terrorism, violence, or incitement Palestinian side agrees to: 1. Continue the program for the collection of illegal weapons 2. Apprehend suspects 3. Forward the list of Palestinian policemen to the Israeli side Release by Israel of Palestinian prisoners
Protocol Concerning the Safe Passage Between the West Bank and Gaza Strip	Oct. 5, 1999		Israel will ensure safe passage between the West Bank and Gaza for persons and transportation during daylight hours
Camp David Negotiations	July 2000	Discussions centered on such issues as: Israeli bases, patrols, and early warning stations in the Jordan Valley and along the Jordanian border Return of refugees and compensation Status of Jerusalem Israeli settlements Territorial division	

Agreement/Proposal	Date	International Security Issues	Palestinian Domestic Security Issues
Taba Negotiations	Jan. 2001	Discussions centered on such issues as: Status of Jerusalem, Return of refugees and compensation, Early warning stations in Palestinian territory, Military capability of a Palestinian state, Israeli settlements, Territorial division	
Mitchell Plan	April 30, 2001	Israelis are concerned about an international force because it might be unresponsive to Israeli security concerns and interfere with bilateral negotiations to settle the conflict	PA and Israel should identify, condemn, and discourage incitement; PA should make clear through concrete action that terrorism is reprehensible and unacceptable; Israel should freeze all settlement activity; Israel should adopt nonlethal responses to unarmed demonstrators; PA should renew cooperation with Israeli security agencies to ensure that Palestinian workers employed within Israel are fully vetted and free of connections to organizations and individuals engaged in terrorism
Tenet Cease-Fire Plan	June 14, 2001	Hold immediate senior-level meeting of Israeli, Palestinian, and U.S. security officials, and reconvene at least once a week; Provide U.S.-supplied videoconferencing to senior-level Israeli and Palestinian officials to facilitate frequent dialogue and security cooperation; Palestinian and Israeli security officials will use the security committee to provide each other, as well as designated U.S. officials, with terrorist threat information	Reinvigorate Israeli-Palestinian district coordination offices; PA will undertake preemptive operations against terrorists, terrorist safe houses, arms depots, and mortar factories

Agreement/Proposal	Date	International Security Issues	Palestinian Domestic Security Issues
Saudi Peace Initiative	March 28, 2002	Achieve a full Israeli withdrawal from all territories occupied since 1967 Achieve a just solution to the Palestinian refugee problem Accept a sovereign independent Palestinian state with East Jerusalem as its capital Arab countries will consider the Arab-Israeli conflict ended and enter into a peace agreement with Israel Arab countries will establish normal relations with Israel	
Performance-Based Roadmap	April 30, 2003	Palestinian leadership issues unequivocal statement reiterating Israeli's right to exist Israeli leadership issues an unequivocal statement affirming its commitment to a two-state solution Quartet representatives begin informal monitoring and consult with parties to establish a formal monitoring mechanism Arab states cut off public and private funding for terrorist groups	Palestinians must undertake visible efforts on the ground to arrest, disrupt, and restrain individuals and groups involved in terrorism Consolidate all Palestinian security organizations into three services reporting to a Minister of Interior Restructure and retrain Palestinian security forces and IDF counterparts

"Clinton Parameters" (Presented by President Bill Clinton to the Israeli and Palestinian Negotiators on December 23, 2000)[1]

Territory

Based on what I heard, I believe that the solution should be in the mid-90%'s, between 94–96% of the West Bank territory of the Palestinian State.

The land annexed by Israel should be compensated by a land swap of 1–3% in addition to territorial arrangement such as a permanent safe passage.

The parties should also consider the swap of leased land to meet their respective needs. There are creative ways for doing this that should address Palestinian and Israeli needs and concerns.

The Parties should develop a map consistent with the following criteria:

- 80% of the settlers in blocks
- Contiguity
- Minimize annexed areas
- Minimize the number of Palestinians affected

Security

The key to security lies in an international presence that can only be withdrawn by mutual consent. This presence will also monitor the implementation of the agreement between both sides.

---

[1] The following text is quoted from Ross (2004).

My best judgment is that the Israeli withdrawal should be carried out over 36 months while international force is gradually introduced in the area. At the end of this period, a small Israeli presence would remain in fixed locations in the Jordan Valley under the authority of the international force for another 36 months. This period could be reduced in the event of favorable regional developments that diminish the threats to Israel.

On early warning situations, Israel should maintain three facilities in the West Bank with a Palestinian liaison presence. The stations will be subject to review after 10 years with any changes in status to be mutually agreed.

Regarding emergency developments, I understand that you still have to develop a map of relevant areas and routes. But in defining what is an emergency, I propose the following definition:

> Imminent and demonstrable threat to Israel's national security of a military nature requires the activation of a national state of emergency.

Of course, the international forces will need to be notified of any such determination.

On airspace, I suggest that the state of Palestine will have sovereignty over its airspace but that the two sides should work out special arrangements for Israeli training and operational needs.

I understand that the Israeli position is that Palestine should be defined as a "demilitarized state" while the Palestinian side proposes "a state with limited arms." As a compromise, I suggest calling it a "non-militarized state."

This will be consistent with the fact that in addition to a strong Palestinian security force, Palestine will have an international force for border security and deterrence purposes.

Jerusalem and Refugees

I have a sense that the remaining gaps have more to do with formulations than practical realities.

Jerusalem

The general principle is that Arab areas are Palestinian and Jewish ones are Israeli. This would apply to the Old City as well. I urge the two sides to work on maps to create maximum contiguity for both sides.

Regarding the Haram/Temple Mount, I believe that the gaps are not related to practical administration but to the symbolic issues of sovereignty and to finding a way to accord respect to the religious beliefs of both sides.

I know you have been discussing a number of formulations, and you can agree on any of these. I add to these two additional formulations guaranteeing Palestinian effective control over Haram while respecting the conviction of the Jewish people. Regarding either one of these two formulations will be international monitoring to provide mutual confidence.

1. Palestinian sovereignty over the Haram and Israeli sovereignty over "the Western Wall and the space sacred to Judaism of which it is a part" or "the Western Wall and the Holy of Holies of which it is a part." There will be a firm commitment by both not to excavate beneath the Haram or behind the Wall.
2. Palestinian shared sovereignty over the Haram and Israeli sovereignty over the Western Wall and shared functional sovereignty over the issue of excavation under the Haram and behind the Wall as mutual consent would be requested before any excavation can take place.

Refugees

I sense that the differences are more relating to formulations and less to what will happen on a practical level. I believe that Israel is prepared to acknowledge the moral and material suffering caused to the Palestinian people as a result of the 1948 war and the need to assist the international community in addressing the problem.

An international commission should be established to implement all the aspects that flow from your agreement: compensation, resettlement, rehabilitation, etc.

The U.S. is prepared to lead an international effort to help the refugees.

The fundamental gap is on how to handle the concept of the right of return. I know the history of the issue and how hard it will be for the Palestinian leadership to appear to be abandoning this principle.

The Israeli side could simply not accept any reference to right of return that would imply a right to immigrate to Israel in defiance of Israel's sovereign policies on admission or that would threaten the Jewish character of the state.

Any solution must address both needs.

The solution will have to be consistent with the two-state approach that both sides have accepted as the way to end the Palestinian-Israeli conflict: the state of Palestine as the homeland of the Palestinian people and the state of Israel as the homeland of the Jewish people.

Under the two-state solution, the guiding principle should be that the Palestinian state will be the focal point for Palestinians who choose to return to the area without ruling out that Israel will accept some of these refugees.

I believe that we need to adopt a formulation on the right of return to Israel itself but that does not negate the aspiration of the Palestinian people to return to the area.

In light of the above, I propose two alternatives:

1. Both sides recognize the right of Palestinian refugees to return to Historic Palestine. Or,
2. Both sides recognize the right of the Palestinian refuges to return to their homeland.

The agreement will define the implementation of this general right in a way that is consistent with the two-state solution. It would list five possible final homes for the refugees:

- The state of Palestine
- Areas in Israel being transferred to Palestine in the land swap
- Rehabilitation in a host country
- Resettlement in a third country
- Admission to Israel

In listing these options, the agreement will make clear that the return to the West Bank, Gaza Strip, and the areas acquired in the land swap would be a right to all Palestinian refugees.

While rehabilitation in host countries, resettlement in third world countries and absorption into Israel will depend upon the policies of those countries.

Israel could indicate in the agreement that it intends to establish a policy so that some of the refugees would be absorbed into Israel consistent with Israel's sovereign decision.

I believe that priority should be given to the refugee population in Lebanon.

The parties would agree that this implements Resolution 194.

I propose that the agreement clearly mark the end of the conflict and its implementation put an end to all its claims. This could be implemented through a UN Security-Council Resolution that notes that Resolutions 242 and 338 have been implemented through the release of Palestinian prisoners.

I believe that this is an outline of a fair and lasting agreement.

It gives the Palestinian people the ability to determine the future on their own land, a sovereign and viable state recognized by the international community, Al-Qods as its capital, sovereignty over the Haram, and new lives for the refugees.

It gives the people of Israel a genuine end to the conflict, real security, the preservation of sacred religious ties, the incorporation of 80% of the settlers into Israel, and the largest Jewish Jerusalem in history recognized by all as its capital.

This is the best I can do. Brief your leaders and tell me if they are prepared to come for discussions based on these ideas. If so, I would meet the next week separately. If not, I have taken this as far as I can.

These are my ideas. If they are not accepted, they are not just off the table, they also go with me when I leave the office.

Bibliography

Agreement on the Gaza Strip and the Jericho Area, The Governments of the State of Israel and the Palestine Liberation Organization, May 4, 1994. Online at www.mfa.gov.il/mfa/go.asp?MFAH00q20 (as of November 2005).

"American Bridging Proposal," *Ha'aretz*, December 25, 2000.

The Aqaba Summit: Statement by Prime Minister Ariel Sharon, June 4, 2003. Online at www.jewishvirtuallibrary.org/jsource/Peace/sharon.html (as of November 2005).

Ben Ami, Shlomo, *Hazit lelo oref: masa el gevulot tahalikh ha-shalom*, Tel Aviv: Yediot aharonot, 2004.

Bennet, James, "No Peace in Sight, Israelis Trust in a Wall," *New York Times*, December 17, 2002, p. A1.

Canadian Department of Foreign Affairs and International Trade, *Non-Paper: Military Components of an International Presence in the Middle East*, Ottawa: Canadian Department of Foreign Affairs and International Trade, January 2003.

Clinton, William Jefferson, "Proposals for a Final Settlement," December 23, 2000, in *Journal of Palestine Studies*, Vol. 30, No. 3, Spring 2001, p. 172.

Declaration of Principles on Interim Self-Government Arrangements, U.S. Embassy in Israel, September 1993. Online at www.usembassy-israel.org.il/publish/peace/peaindex.htm#oslo (as of November 2005).

de Hoop Scheffer, Jaap, *Speech by NATO Secretary General Jaap de Hoop Scheffer*, February 24, 2005. Online at www.nato.int/docu/speech/2005/s050224a.htm (as of November 2005).

Devi, Sharmila, "Israeli Wall Drives the Palestinians to Despair," *Financial Times*, February 22, 2003, p. 5.

Diehl, Paul F., "Peacekeeping and the Quest for Peace," *Political Science Quarterly*, Vol. 103, No. 3, Autumn 1988, pp. 485–507.

Elizur, Yuval, "Israel Banks on a Fence," *Foreign Affairs*, Vol. 82, No. 2, March/April 2003, pp. 106–119.

The Europa World Yearbook 2002, London: Europa Publications, 2002.

Foundation for Middle East Peace, *Israeli Settlements in the Occupied Territories: A Guide,* Washington, D.C.: Foundation for Middle East Peace, March 2002.

The Fourth Geneva Convention, Article 49, Paragraph 6. Online at www.jewishvirtuallibrary. org/jsource/History/Human_Rights/geneva1.html (as of November 2005).

Glaser, Charles L., "Realists as Optimists: Cooperation as Self-Help," *International Security,* Vol. 19, No. 3, Winter 1994/95, pp. 50–90.

————, "The Security Dilemma Revisited," *World Politics,* Vol. 50, No. 1, October 1997, pp. 171–201.

Hanieh, Akram, "The Camp David Papers," Special Document in *Journal of Palestine Studies,* Vol. 30, No. 2, Winter 2001, pp. 75–97.

Helping a Palestinian State Succeed: Key Findings, Santa Monica, Calif.: RAND Corporation, MG-146/1-RC, 2005.

Herz, John, "Idealist Internationalism and the Security Dilemma," *World Politics,* Vol. 2, No. 2, January 1950, pp. 157–180.

Higgins, Rosalyn, *United Nations Peacekeeping, Volume I: The Middle East,* London: Oxford University Press, 1969, pp. 335–367.

Hillen, John, *Blue Helmets: The Strategy of UN Military Operations,* Washington, D.C.: Brassey's, 1998.

Howard, Michael, and Robert Hunter, *Israel and the Arab World: The Crisis of 1967,* Adelphi Paper #41, London: Institute for Strategic Studies, September 1967.

Hroub, Khaled, *Hamas: Political Thought and Practice,* Institute for Palestine Studies, October 2000.

The Israeli Information Center for Human Rights in the Occupied Territories. Online at www. btselem.org (as of November 2005).

Israeli-Palestinian Interim Agreement on the West Bank and the Gaza Strip, September 28, 1995. Online at www.soas.ac.uk/Centres/IslamicLaw/AIIA.html (as of November 2005).

Jane's Terrorism and Insurgency Centre. Online at http://jtic.janes.com (as of November 2005).

Jervis, Robert, "Cooperation Under the Security Dilemma," *World Politics,* Vol. 30, No. 2, January 1978, pp. 167–214.

Keinon, Herb, "Sharon to Call for Removal of Outposts at Aqaba," *Jerusalem Post,* June 2, 2003, p. 1.

Khalidi, Rashid, "The Centrality of Jerusalem to an End of Conflict Agreement," *Journal of Palestine Studies,* Vol. 30, No. 3, Spring 2001, pp. 83–87.

Kydd, Andrew, "Sheep in Sheep's Clothing: Why Security Seekers Do Not Fight Each Other," *Security Studies,* Vol. 7, No. 1, Autumn 1997, pp. 1114–1154.

Lazaroff, Tovah, "Fence to Separate Rachel's Tomb from Bethlehem," *Jerusalem Post,* February 19, 2003, p. 2.

Lein, Yehezkel, *The Separation Barrier: Position Paper,* Jerusalem: B'Tselem, 2002.

———, "Terror from Damascus, Part I," *Peacewatch,* No. 420, May 7, 2003.

Levitt, Matthew, "Palestinian Islamic Jihad: Getting By with a Little Help from Its Friends," *Peacewatch,* No. 396, September 3, 2002.

Luft, Gal, "The Mirage of a Demilitarized Palestine," *Middle East Quarterly,* Summer 2001. Online at www.meforum.org/article/112 (as of November 2005).

Malley, Robert, and Hussein Agha, "Camp David: The Tragedy of Errors," *The New York Review of Books,* Vol. 48, No. 13, August 9, 2001, pp. 62–63.

Mishal, Shaul, and Avraham Sela, *The Palestinian Hamas: Vision, Violence and Coexistence,* New York: Columbia University Press, 2000.

"The Moratinos Nonpaper on the Taba Negotiations," *Journal of Palestine Studies,* Vol. 31, No. 3, Spring 2002, pp. 81–89.

The Oslo II Agreement, September 28, 1995. Online at www.acpr.org.il/resources/oslo2.html (as of November 2005).

Pew Research Center for the People and the Press, *Views of a Changing World: June 2003 Survey Report,* Washington, D.C.: Pew Research Center for the People and the Press, June 2003.

PLO Negotiating Team, "Reservations Concerning President Bill Clinton's 23 December Proposals for an Israeli-Palestinian Peace Agreement," January 1, 2001, *Journal of Palestine Studies,* Vol. 30, No. 3, Spring 2001, pp. 155–159.

Quandt, William B., *Peace Process: American Diplomacy and the Arab-Israeli Conflict Since 1967,* Washington, D.C.: Brookings Institutions Press, 2001a.

———, "Clinton and the Arab-Israeli Conflict: The Limits of Incrementalism," *Journal of Palestine Studies,* Vol. 30, No. 2, Winter 2001b, pp. 26–40.

The RAND Palestinian State Study Team, *Building a Successful Palestinian State,* Santa Monica, Calif.: RAND Corporation, MG-146-DCR, 2005.

Report of the Sharm el-Sheikh Fact-Finding Committee (The Mitchell Report), April 30, 2001. Online at www.al-bab.com/arab/docs/pal/mitchell1.htm (as of November 2005).

Ross, Dennis, *The Missing Peace,* New York: Farrar, Straus and Giroux, 2004.

Safran, Nadav, *From War to War: The Arab-Israeli Confrontation, 1948–1967,* Indianapolis: Pegasus, 1969.

Schoenbaum, Michael, Adel K. Afifi, and Richard J. Deckelbaum, *Strengthening the Palestinian Health System,* Santa Monica, Calif.: RAND Corporation, MG-311-1-DCR, 2005.

Schweller, Randall L., "Neorealism's Status-Quo Bias: What Security Dilemma?" *Security Studies,* Vol. 5, No. 3, Spring 1996, pp. 90–121.

Sharm el-Sheikh Fact-Finding Committee, *First Statement of the Government of Israel, Israeli Ministry of Foreign Affairs,* December 28, 2000. Online at www.mfa.gov.il/mfa/go.asp?MFAH0jcc0 (as of November 2005).

Smith, Charles D., *Palestine and the Arab-Israeli Conflict, Third Edition,* New York: St. Martin's Press, 1996.

Sontag, Susan, "Quest for Middle East Peace," *New York Times,* July 26, 2001, p. A1.

Stacy, William E., *U.S. Army Border Operation in Germany, 1945–1983,* Heidelberg, Germany: Headquarters, U.S. Army Europe, 1984.

Suisman, Doug, Steven N. Simon, Glenn E. Robinson, C. Ross Anthony, and Michael Schoenbaum, *The Arc: A Formal Structure for a Palestinian State,* Santa Monica, Calif.: RAND Corporation, MG-327-GG, 2005.

TIME Magazine, posted Sunday, June 9, 2002. Online at www.time.com/time/covers/1101020617/story.html (as of November 2005).

Toameh, Khaled Abu, "Uniform Culture," *The Jerusalem Report,* July 31, 2000, p. 28.

Treaty of Peace Between the State of Israel and the Hashemite Kingdom of Jordan, October 26, 1994. Online at www.us-israel.org/jsource/Peace/isrjor.html (as of November 2005).

United Nations, *The Blue Helmets,* New York: United Nations, 1990.

UNSCO (Office of the United Nations Special Coordinator in the Occupied Territories), *The Impact of Closure and Other Mobility Restrictions on Palestinian Productive Activities,* New York: UNSCO, 2002.

U.S. Department of State, *Patterns of Global Terrorism, 2002,* Washington, D.C.: U.S. Department of State, 2003a.

———, "A Performance-Based Roadmap to a Permanent Two-State Solution to the Israeli-Palestinian Conflict," Office of the Spokesman, April 30, 2003b. Online at www.state.gov/r/pa/prs/ps/2003/20062.htmwww.un.org/media/main/roadmap122002.html (as of November 2005).

U.S. Department of State Bulletin, September 1982.